OXFORD PROGRESSIVE ENGLISH READERS

Frankenstein

Frankenstein

Mary Shelley

HONG KONG

OXFORD UNIVERSITY PRESS 1979

KUALA LUMPUR SINGAPORE TOKYO

Oxford University Press

OXFORD LONDON GLASGOW
NEW YORK TORONTO MELBOURNE WELLINGTON
KUALA LUMPUR SINGAPORE HONG KONG TOKYO
DELHI BOMBAY CALCUTTA MADRAS KARACHI
NAIROBI DAR ES SALAAM CAPE TOWN

© *Oxford University Press 1979*

ISBN 0 19 581234 4

Retold by J. Alderson. Illustrated by Carol Owen

Printed by Sun Fung Printing Co. 16 Westlands Rd., Melbourne Ind. Bldg., H.K. Published by Oxford University Press, News Building, North Point, Hong Kong.

Contents

		Page
	Letters Written by Robert Walton to His Sister, Margaret	1
1	The Early Life of Frankenstein	6
2	Frankenstein Becomes a Scientist	8
3	The Monster Is Created	11
4	The Calm Before the Storm	15
5	Murder	17
6	The Night of the Storm	20
7	The Trial of Justine	24
8	In the Death Cell	26
9	Return of the Demon	29
10	The Monster's First Experiences	32
11	The Monster Meets Man	34
12	The Monster Receives an Education	35
13	The Monster Shows Himself to the Cottagers	38
14	The Monster Becomes Filled with Hate	42
15	The Monster's Good Deed	44
16	The Monster's Revenge	46
17	The Promise	48
18	Frankenstein Travels to England	51
19	Curse of the Demon	54
20	Burial at Sea	57
21	A Dreadful Shock	62
22	Fever	64
23	The Marriage	67
24	The Monster Keeps His Promise	71
25	The Demon Escapes	75
26	The Long Chase	77
	Letters Written by Robert Walton to His Sister, Margaret	80
	Questions	86

OXFORD PROGRESSIVE ENGLISH READERS

The best of modern fiction and the classics is available in the OPER series, in an abridged and simplified form, to students of English as a second or foreign language.

The series is divided into four grades of difficulty. In grade 1 vocabulary is restricted to 1,900 head words, in grade 2 to 2,900 head words, in grade 3 to 3,500 head words and in grade 4 to 5,000 head words.

Grade 4 is intended for students who are not quite ready to read texts in the original. The stories are rewritten in clear modern English. Idiom is kept to a minimum and difficult words are explained in footnotes. To encourage students to read outside the classroom, grade 4 OPERs have been designed to look more adult and less like school texts than the lower grades of the series.

Letters Written by Robert Walton
to His Sister, Margaret

St. Petersburg, Dec. 11th

My dearest Margaret,

You will be very glad to know that I am safe, in spite of all your fears. I arrived yesterday and feel very confident about my expedition to the North Pole.

London is a long way off. I am now walking the streets of St. Petersburg. A cold northern wind blows upon my cheeks. This fills me with delight. Do you understand this feeling, my sweet sister? This wind has come from the North Pole itself and makes me dream of that marvellous land of ice and snow. It is no good people telling me that the pole is the place of frost or a freezing desert full of loneliness. In my imagination, it is a place of beauty and delight. There, the sun never sets and I may be able to discover the wonderful power which attracts the needles of compasses. I will be treading in places where no human being has trod before. Danger or death mean nothing to me now. I feel the same joy and excitement a little boy feels when he gets into a tiny boat with some holiday friends and sets out to explore a nearby river.

Six years have passed since I first decided to make this expedition. I began to strengthen my body in order to stand up to hardships. I went with whale-fishers on several expeditions to the North Sea. I learned to conquer thirst, great hunger and lack of sleep. I spent all my nights studying medicine and science so that I might be able to cope with any danger or difficulty.

I shall hire a boat and employ some men who have had experience of whale fishing. Then I shall set sail in June when the weather will be at its most favourable. One day, God willing, I shall return. In the meantime, farewell, my dear, excellent Margaret. God bless you. I will always remember your love and kindness.

Your affectionate brother,
Robert Walton.

July 7th

My dear sister,

I am quickly writing a few lines to say that I am safe and well on the way to the North Pole. This letter will reach England on a merchantship now on its homeward journey from Russia. I am in good spirits, and my men are brave and loyal. They are not even frightened by the huge sheets of ice that are beginning to float by.

So far, everything has gone wonderfully well. I will not take any foolish risks, but I am more than ever determined to succeed. I must finish writing now as there is so much work to do.

Heaven bless you, my sister,

Robert

August 5th

A very strange event has taken place. I must keep a written record of it, even though there is no way, at the moment, of sending these letters to you.

Last Monday we were almost completely surrounded by ice. It had closed in on us from all sides and there was hardly any water in which the ship would float. Things were beginning to look dangerous, especially as we were also surrounded by a very thick fog. We decided to wait patiently and hope that some change would take place in the weather.

About two o'clock, the mist cleared away. We could see huge and uneven plains of ice stretching out in every direction. They seemed endless and some of my companions groaned with despair. I, too, was beginning to be worried when a strange sight suddenly attracted our attention. We saw a low carriage fixed on a sledge and drawn by dogs. It was about half a mile away and heading northwards. The driver who guided the dogs had the shape of a man but was as tall as a giant. With our telescopes, we watched the speedy progress of this traveller until he was lost amongst the distant slopes of the ice.

We were absolutely amazed by this sight. As far as we knew, we were many hundreds of miles away from any land. Several of the men wanted to follow his track but I refused to give them permission. It would have been far too dangerous.

About two hours after this event, we heard the sea move beneath the ship. Before night the ice broke and we were free. However, we decided to remain where we were. It was dark and we were afraid of crashing into huge masses of ice which were beginning to float all around us. I took advantage of this delay and went to rest for a few hours.

In the morning, I went up on deck. It was daylight. All the sailors were crowded on one side of the ship. They were apparently talking to someone in the sea. I looked down and saw a sledge. It was similar to the one we had seen the day before. It had floated towards us during the night on a large fragment of ice. Only one of the dogs was left alive. Some were lying dead on the ice, others had obviously fallen into the sea. Inside the sledge, however, was a human being. The sailors were trying to persuade him to enter our ship. This man was a European. He did not look anything like that other traveller we had seen the day before. When I appeared on deck, the first mate said, 'Here is our captain. We will not allow you to die in the middle of this sea.'

When he saw me, the stranger decided to talk. He spoke English with a foreign accent. 'Before I come on board your ship,' he said, 'would you please tell me where you are going?'

I was amazed by his question! When the ice melted, this man would sink beneath the deep, cold waters! I would have thought our ship would have been more precious to him than all the gold and silver in the entire universe. However, I remembered my manners and told him we were headed towards the North Pole.

Upon hearing this, he seemed satisfied and agreed to come aboard. Good God! If you could have seen this man, Margaret, you would have been as shocked as I was. He looked dreadful! His arms and legs were frozen and his body was almost a skeleton. I had never seen a man in such a terrible condition. We carried him below into a cabin, but as soon as he was removed from the fresh air he fainted. We had to bring him back to the deck. There we restored him to life by rubbing him with brandy and forcing him to swallow a small amount. Next we wrapped him up in blankets. Then we placed him near the chimney of the kitchen stove. Gradually he recovered and ate a little soup.

Two days passed before this man was strong enough to speak. I had great trouble stopping the men from bothering him with their questions. Once, however, the first mate asked him why he had come so far over the ice in his sledge.

The stranger's face became very sad and he replied, 'I must find the one who runs away from me.'

'Was he travelling in the same way as yourself?'

'Yes,' he replied.

We told the stranger about the giant. This made him very excited and he asked us lots of questions. He wanted to know in which direction 'the demon' had set off. He wanted to know if I thought the breaking up of the ice might have destroyed the other sledge. He kept wanting to go up on deck to look for signs of wreckage, but we forced him to remain inside as his health was still very bad.

August 13th

The stranger and I have become friends. He is a gentleman and all the crew admire him. During one of our conversations, he asked me why I wanted to find the North Pole. I became very excited. I told him that I had a hunger for adventure and knowledge. I told him that I was prepared to sacrifice my fortune and my entire life if I could only discover something about the strange and mysterious world in which we live.

As I said this, the man's face suddenly became filled with great sadness. He held his hands to his face and tears began to trickle through his fingers. A groan burst from his body and he said, 'Unhappy man! I too am a kind of explorer. I suffered from your kind of madness. You must not destroy yourself and others in your search for knowledge. Let me tell you my story before it is too late. You must learn from my mistakes!'

I thanked the stranger for his kindness. With his permission, I am to write down the details of his story whenever my duties allow. As I write, his voice seems to ring in my ears. I can see his eyes and his thin hands tremble with emotion. In some ways he reminds me of a ship that has been wrecked by a fierce storm. His story must have been truly strange and terrible to have caused him so much suffering.

1   The Early Life of Frankenstein

My name is Victor Frankenstein. I was born in Switzerland and my family was rich and very respectable. It may seem strange, but my childhood was very happy. My parents loved me deeply. They looked upon me as an innocent and helpless creature who had been sent to them from heaven.

For a long time I was their only child. Then my parents moved to Italy. It was here that my mother met a family of peasants. They were starving and could not afford to feed all their children. We looked at the little boys and girls very closely. They were all dark-skinned except one. This was a girl with beautiful golden hair and blue eyes. My mother wanted to adopt her and the peasant woman was delighted. She said the child was not her own. She had herself adopted it from an Italian nobleman who had been arrested and killed for fighting against the government.

When my father returned to the house, he was delighted. The girl was called Elizabeth and we all loved her. She became like a sister to me and we were brought up together.

Two years later my mother gave birth to another son and this child was called William. My father decided to give up travelling and we settled down in Switzerland near Lake Geneva.

As I grew older, I became very interested in science. I wanted to learn all the secrets of nature. I wanted to discover how to turn ordinary metals into gold and silver. Also, I wanted to discover a way of making people live forever. If only this could be possible!

I became interested in magic. I muttered strange rhymes and tried to conjure up* ghosts and devils from the land of the dead. Elizabeth was horrified by all this. She did not

*conjure up, cause to appear

want to know the secrets of nature. She was only interested in the beauty of nature. She spent most of her time reading poetry or walking through fields and gazing at the loveliness of the snow-capped mountains.

One day, a violent and terrible thunderstorm shook our house. This event was to change my life. The storm came from behind the mountains and bursts of thunder seemed to come from all over the sky. The noise terrified Elizabeth and she ran back into the house. I stood by the door and watched. I was filled with curiosity and excitement. Suddenly, a stream of fire seemed to explode out of an old and beautiful oak tree twenty yards away. When the dazzling light vanished, I noticed that the oak had disappeared. Nothing remained but a blackened stump. Next morning we had a closer look at the tree. It had been torn into tiny strips of wood. I had never seen anything so completely destroyed.

As a result of this storm, I became interested in the laws of electricity. I decided I would go to university and study science. If only that storm had never happened!

D A terrible thunderstorm destroyed a true, it had been torn into tiny strips of wood, its it made Frankenstein intested in electricity.

2   Frankenstein Becomes a Scientist

Just before I was to go to Ingoldstadt University my mother died. This was to be the first of many dreadful events which were to poison my life.

Elizabeth had caught scarlet fever. My mother had looked after her like an angel and the girl's life was saved. Two days later, my mother became sick with the same fever and died. On her deathbed, she joined the hands of Elizabeth and myself together.

'My children,' she said, 'I had hoped to see you married. For the sake of your poor father, you must promise to become man and wife one day. Elizabeth, my love, you must be William's mother now. One of these days I hope to meet you again in another world.'

She died peacefully and Elizabeth became a wonderful mother to William. Several weeks later, I set off for Ingoldstadt. My father was there to bless me. My boyhood friend, Clerval, shook me by the hand. And Elizabeth begged me to write to her as often as possible. My heart was filled with a sweet kind of sadness as the coach took me away from the happy place of my childhood.

Several hours later, I saw the high, white steeple* of the town. I stepped out of the coach and was shown to the small room which was to be my study.

I was not very happy at the university. The only man I really liked and respected was a professor called Mr Waldman. He was about fifty years old and had a kind-looking face. He was small but his body was straight and his voice was one of the most pleasant I had ever heard. To this very day I can hear the words he spoke in a lecture on modern chemistry, 'Times have changed,' he said. 'These days we know that

*steeple, tall, pointed part of a building, usually a church.

ordinary metals cannot be turned into gold. We know that the fountain of youth is just a dream. The modern scientist spends all his time in a laboratory gazing through a microscope or staring into a test tube. And yet he has performed miracles. He has found out how nature works. He has climbed up into the clouds. He has discovered how the blood flows around the body. He knows all about the air we breathe. Modern scientists have become the new masters of the world.'

That night I could not sleep. I kept hearing his words again and again. So much had been achieved by science. I would achieve more. I would become an explorer. I would discover the secret of life itself!

I studied all day and all night. Two years passed. I learned how the human body worked. I went into graveyards at night and dug up corpses. I was not afraid. Stories about ghosts and demons had never made me tremble in the slightest. As far as I was concerned, a churchyard was simply a place where dead bodies were buried. I felt great pity for those people whose beauty and strength had been turned into food for the worm. Night after night I examined dead bodies. I examined their eyes and their brains.

One day a sudden light broke in upon me. It was a light so brilliant and wonderful that I became dizzy. I had finally managed to discover the astonishing secret of life!

I can see by the surprise in your eyes and your eagerness that you too hope to learn of my secret. But I will never tell you. Such knowledge has destroyed my life. I will not allow it to destroy yours.

I had discovered the secret of life. Now I needed to build a body to receive this precious gift. This was to prove very difficult. The human body is an extremely complicated piece of work. There are so many fibres, muscles and veins. There are so many things which can go wrong. I spent several months collecting together my materials and then I began.

I worked very hard. I felt I was doing something wonderful for the world in which I lived. A new race of human beings would bless me for having created them. I imagined that one day I might even be able to bring the dead back to life.

In fact, I was working too hard. My face had turned white and my body had wasted away owing to lack of proper food and exercise. Time after time I kept failing. The moon gazed down on me as I worked throughout the night. Sweat poured from my face as I went about my task. Can you imagine the horrors I had to face? I dug about in damp graves and tortured living animals as part of my experiments. My arms and legs began to tremble. My eyes seemed to go dizzy as I remembered some of the dreadful things I had done. Despite all this, I kept working like a demon. I visited burial places and tore dead bodies apart with my bare hands. I collected bones and pieces of flesh and kept them in a room at the top of a house. This was my workshop, filled with all kinds of horrors. At times it looked like the filthy kitchen of a cannibal*. My eyeballs were beginning to bulge from their sockets. To obtain my materials I robbed rooms where medical students cut up corpses and even visited places where animals are killed for meat.

As I worked, the summer passed me by. It was the most beautiful season. The harvest was magnificent and the vines were full of juicy grapes. But my eyes were blind to the charms of nature. I knew my family were worried about me, but they left me in peace.

Every night I was ill with a kind of slow fever. I became so nervous that the fall of a leaf made me jump. I avoided my fellow men as if I had committed some sort of crime. At times I became frightened of the wreck I had become. I hoped that my work would soon end and that exercise and amusement would drive away my illness.

*cannibal, man who eats human flesh.

3 The Monster Is Created

On a dreary night in November I finally finished my task. I collected all my instruments around me so that I might send a spark of life into the creature that lay by my feet. It was already one o'clock in the morning. The rain pattered against the window panes and my candle was nearly burned out. Suddenly, in the dim light, I saw the dull yellow eye of the creature open! It breathed hard and a tremendous shudder moved through its body.

How can I describe my feelings when this happened? How can I describe the wretch I had taken so long to create? His body was perfectly shaped and I had chosen his features so as to make him beautiful. Beautiful! Great God! The experiment had taken so long that I had not been able to preserve certain parts of his flesh. His yellow skin hardly covered the workings of the muscles and arteries beneath. His hair was shiny, black and long. His teeth were as white as pearls. But this beauty only formed a more horrid contrast with his watery eyes. His skin was shrivelled and his lips were straight and black with decay.

My feelings had suddenly changed. For two years I had worked like a slave in order to bring life to such a creature. Now that I had finished, the beauty of my dream vanished. My heart was filled with horror and disgust. I could not bear the sight of the being I had created. I rushed out of the room and spent hours walking about in my bedchamber. A thousand twisted thoughts swept through my mind. My mental sufferings were so great I fainted upon my bed. Even then, I was disturbed by the wildest dreams. I thought I saw Elizabeth. She was in the bloom of health, walking in the streets of Ingoldstadt. Delighted and surprised, I threw my arms around her. But as I pressed the first kiss on her lips, they became bright blue with the colour of death. Her face seemed to change and I thought I held the corpse of my dead mother in my arms. A funeral cloak covered her body and I saw worms from the grave crawling in the folds of the cloth. I woke from my faint in horror. A cold dampness covered my forehead. My teeth chattered and every part of my body began to shake. The dim and yellow light of the moon forced its way through the shutters. It was then that I saw the miserable monster I had created. He held up the curtain of the bed and what were supposed to be his eyes were fixed upon me. His jaws opened and he muttered strange, shapeless sounds. A grin wrinkled his cheeks. Perhaps he might have spoken but I did not hear. He stretched out a hand as if to hold me back but I escaped and rushed downstairs. I spent the rest of the night in the courtyard next to the house. I walked up and down for hours clenching my fists and tearing my hair. Every time I heard a noise I looked around me, expecting to catch sight of that demon-like corpse to which I had given the gift of life.

No human being could look upon that horrid face! Even a very old corpse brought to life could not be so ugly. I had often looked at him while he was still unfinished. He had been ugly then, but when the spark of life had flowed through him he had looked like a creature straight out of hell. Worst of all, I had made him a giant. He was about eight feet tall and must surely possess tremendous strength.

During the night, my heart was beating so quickly I could feel every vein bursting with my blood. At other times I was so exhausted and weak I almost fell to the ground. Apart from being horrified, I was bitterly disappointed. All my beautiful dreams had turned into nightmares and I felt ashamed.

Morning came. It was wet and miserable. My aching eyes could see the church of Ingoldstadt. I could see its white steeple and clock. The porter opened the gates of the court and I ran from that place. For me it had been like a madhouse during the night! I raced through the streets, expecting to meet that creature at every corner. Rain began to pour

down from a black and comfortless sky.

Soon after, I found myself outside the house of Henry Clerval, my boyhood friend.

'My dear Victor,' he said, 'I am delighted to see you, but whatever is the matter? You are soaked and you look ill.'

I told him that I had been working too hard and had got caught out in the rain. My friend immediately ordered a carriage and took me back to the very place from which I had escaped! I did not dare tell him about the events of the night before. In any case, he would not have believed me. He would have accused me of being mad.

I trembled violently when we arrived back at my college. Perhaps the creature was still walking about in my room. I was frightened of meeting this monster again, but I simply did not want Henry to see him. I told my friend to remain at the bottom of the stairs and rushed up to my room. I put my hand on the lock of the door and then I hesitated. A cold shiver ran down my spine. Suddenly I threw open the door like a child who expects to see a ghost on the other side, but nothing appeared. I stepped fearfully in. The apartment was empty and the bedroom was also free from the demon. I could hardly believe my good luck. I clapped my hands for joy and ran down to Clerval.

All through breakfast I kept jumping up and down. I clapped my hands and laughed out loud. At first Clerval was amused, but when he looked more closely and saw a strange wildness in my eyes, he became frightened.

'My dear Victor,' he cried, 'what is the matter, for God's sake? Don't laugh like that. You're very ill! What's the cause of all this?'

'Don't ask me!' I screamed, putting my hands in front of my eyes. I thought I could see the dreaded monster glide into the room like a ghost. 'Oh, save me! Save me!' I cried. I was sure that the monster had grabbed me. I struggled furiously and fell down in a fit.

4 The Calm Before the Storm

That incident was the beginning of a long nervous fever. I had to remain in bed for several months. During all this time Henry looked after me. He did not tell my relations how ill I was. He was worried it might shock my sick and aging father or cause unnecessary suffering to the tender-hearted Elizabeth.

Eventually I recovered. I began to notice that the fallen leaves had disappeared. The young buds were shooting out of the trees that shaded my window. It was a heavenly spring and I was almost able to forget the dreadful sight of that living nightmare.

Henry handed me a letter. It was from my cousin Elizabeth. It read as follows:

My dearest Victor,

I know you have been very ill. Nothing would have stopped me from seeing you except that I know Henry is so very reliable and I trust him completely. He tells me you are getting better, so I am sending you this letter.

Get well soon and return to us. We are all happy and cheerful but miss you a great deal, especially your father.

The scenery around the house has not changed. The blue lake and the snow-clad mountains are as beautiful as ever. Only one change has taken place in the house. We have taken on a new servant girl called Justine Moritz. The poor girl's parents died recently and as she was a favourite of one of your aunts I thought it was an excellent idea to employ her. She is very clever and gentle and extremely pretty.

I must also say a few words to you about my cousin, the little darling William. He is very tall for his age and has blue eyes, dark eyelashes and curling hair. When he smiles, two little dimples appear on his cheeks which are rosy with health. He has already had one or two little girlfriends, but Louisa Biron is his favourite. She is a pretty little girl of five years of age.

Please give our thanks to Henry for his kindness and his many letters. We are sincerely grateful. Adieu! my cousin. Take care of yourself and write — one word or one line will be a blessing to us.

Elizabeth.

I wrote immediately. Two weeks later I was able to leave my room and return to the university. However, by this time I had developed a hatred of science. I could not bear to enter a laboratory and the sight of chemical equipment made me tremble with fear. My professors, including Mr Waldman, kept praising me. They told me I was the most brilliant scientist the university had ever produced. They wanted me to begin my studies again, but I refused.

Three months later, I decided I was strong enough to return home. The weather was beautiful. Everyone that Henry and I met seemed full of life and happiness. I was so excited and cheerful I raced my friend back to the college.

I did not realize what dreadful events were soon to happen. This period in my life was to be the calm before the storm.

5   Murder

When we got back to the college, I found the following letter from my father:

My dear Victor,

Soon you will be coming home. You will expect to see us happy and smiling. Instead you will see us full of sorrow. Something dreadful has happened to us and you must prepare yourself to receive the shock.

William is dead. That sweet child who was so happy and gentle is dead. Victor, he was murdered!

I know it will not be possible to comfort you, but I feel you ought to know what happened.

Last Thursday, Elizabeth, William and myself went for a walk in the countryside. We sat down to a picnic. William quickly finished his meal and ran off to play. He did not return.

After a while we became very worried and began a search. The night came. Elizabeth thought he might have gone back to the house so we returned. He was not there. We went back with torches to the scene of the picnic. I was worried that my dear little son might suffer from the cold and the damps of the night. Elizabeth was in a state of shock so I told her to stay at home. At five o'clock in the morning, I discovered my youngest son. Last night he had been happy and full of health. Now he lay stretched out on the grass. His body had changed colour and he did not move. The marks of the murderer's fingers were on his neck.

We took the body home. My face was so sad that Elizabeth guessed the truth. She wanted to see the body. At first I refused to allow this, but she insisted. She entered the room and examined the neck of the victim. Then she clasped her hands and cried, 'O God! I have murdered my darling child!'

She fainted and for a while we feared for her life. When she recovered, she began to weep and sigh. She told me that during the evening of the murder William had persuaded her to let him wear a valuable locket which contained a portrait of your dear dead mother. The locket has gone and this no doubt was what tempted the murderer to do his frightful deed. We are making every effort to find the killer, but this will not bring poor William back to life!

Come to us, dearest Victor. You are the only one who can comfort Elizabeth. She weeps all the time and blames herself for the death of the boy. Her words are breaking my heart. Thank God your dear mother did not live to see the cruel, miserable death of her youngest child!

Come to us, Victor, but do not come with thoughts of hatred and revenge towards the murderer. Come with feelings of peace and gentleness. You must heal the wounds in Elizabeth's mind, not make them worse.

Your loving father,
Alphonse Frankenstein

Clerval watched me read this letter. He was surprised to see my face turn from joy to despair. I threw the letter on the table and covered my face with my hands.

'My dear Frankenstein,' exclaimed Henry. 'Why are you always unhappy? My dear friend, what has happened?'

I pointed to the letter and walked up and down as Clerval read it.

'I can't offer you any comfort,' he said, putting the letter down. 'Nothing can bring William back to life. What do you intend to do?'

'I will go instantly to Geneva. Come with me, Henry, to order the horses.'

During our walk, Clerval did in fact try to say a few words of comfort. 'Poor William!' he said. 'The little child now sleeps with his mother. How dreadful that such an innocent child should feel the cruel grasp of a murderer! Poor little fellow! We have only one comfort. His friends will mourn

and weep, but he is at rest. The pain is over, his sufferings
are at an end forever. The grass covers his gentle body and
he knows no more pain. We need pity him no longer. Instead,
we must show our pity for those who loved him and are still
alive.'

Clerval spoke these words as we hurried through the streets.
The words impressed themselves in my mind and I remembered them when I was alone. But now, as soon as the horses
arrived, I hurried into a carriage and said goodbye to my
friend.

6   The Night of the Storm

My journey was very sad. At first I wanted to get to my relatives as quickly as possible. Then I began to slow down as I got nearer to my home town. I was feeling very confused. I was frightened and I did not know the reason why. I stopped by the side of the lake and stared at it for hours.

Night began to fall. I could hardly see the dark mountains and I felt more and more depressed. I felt there was evil all around. I felt I was to become the most miserable of all human beings. Alas! I was to be proved right.

It was completely dark when I arrived outside the town of Geneva. The gates were shut so I had to spend the night in a small village about a mile away. I tried to sleep but I felt restless. As the sky looked peaceful, I decided to visit the spot where poor William had been murdered. I took a small boat and began to row across the lake. As I did so, I noticed the lightning playing on the summit of Mont Blanc. It was a strange and beautiful sight. The storm came closer and closer. I landed and climbed up a small hill to watch. It moved nearer and nearer. The heavens were covered with clouds. I felt the rain coming in large drops. It fell slowly at first, then it became faster and more violent.

I began to walk back to the boat. The darkness and the storm increased every minute. Thunder burst with a terrific crash over my head. It made an echo in the distant mountains. My eyes were dazzled by vivid flashes of lightning. The lake was lit up and looked like a vast sheet of fire. Then for a moment everything seemed pitch black until the eye recovered itself from the effects of the flash. As is usual in Switzerland, the storm seemed to explode in different parts of the sky at the same moment.

This magnificent war in the sky made me clench my fists with excitement. I opened my mouth and shouted out aloud,

'William, my brother! This music is for your funeral. The gods are sad and angry!'

As I said these words, I saw a figure appear from the darkness. It had come from a clump of trees nearby. I stood absolutely still and watched with horror. I could not be mistaken. A flash of lightning lit up the object. I could see its shape clearly now. It was the size of a giant and the face was horribly deformed. I knew at once that it was the filthy demon to whom I had given life. What was he doing there? Was he the murderer of my brother? The minute that idea come into my mind I realized it was the truth. My teeth chattered and I was forced to lean against a tree for support. The figure passed me quickly and I lost it in the darkness.

He was the murderer! I could not doubt it. I thought of chasing the monster but I knew I stood no chance of catching him. There was another flash of lightning. I saw the creature hanging from the steep rocks of a small mountain. In no time at all, he reached the top and disappeared.

I could not move. It was as if I had been turned into stone. The thunder stopped but the rain continued to pour down. Darkness surrounded everything. My mind was like a whirlpool. Almost a year had passed since the night that demon had first received life. Perhaps he had committed other crimes! I had created a monster, a murderer who delighted in blood and misery.

I spent the rest of that cold, wet night in the open air. My mind began to play tricks. I felt that this creature was like my own evil spirit which was going to destroy everything that I loved.

Day came. I found the boat and rowed back across the lake. Soon I was walking through the open gates of the town towards my father's house. I wanted to tell everybody about the murderer and organize a search party. Then I thought about the story I would have to tell the police. Would they believe that I had met a monster at the foot of a mountain? Would they believe that I had created this monster myself? I remembered the nervous fever that had kept me in bed for several months and the way I had raved in terror. They would say I was mad. They would lock me up in a madhouse and I would stay there forever. Even if they sent out a search party, they would never catch the monster. Who could possibly catch a creature capable of climbing steep cliffs and mountains? Thoughts such as these made me decide to say nothing about the monster.

It was about five o'clock in the morning when I entered my father's house. I told the servants not to disturb the family and went upstairs to the library. Over the fireplace, there was a picture of my mother kneeling by the coffin of her dead father. Below this was a small picture of William. Once again my eyes became wet with tears and a cold shiver crept down my back.

Presently my father entered. He tried to smile at me, but I saw that his face was filled with sorrow and I knew that the shock must have come close to killing him.

'Welcome, my dearest Victor,' he said. 'What a pity you couldn't have come earlier when William was still alive and the house was filled with joy. I hope you can comfort Elizabeth. She keeps blaming herself for the death of William. However, now that the murderer has been discovered——'

I was amazed. 'You've got the murderer! Good God! how can that be? Who could have caught him? It's impossible. It would be like overtaking the wind or drinking a mountain stream with a straw. I saw him too. He was free last night.'

My father stared at me and shook his head. He acted as if he thought I was still sick with the fever. 'I don't understand you,' he said. 'The murderer is a woman!'

'A woman!'

'Yes,' he said. 'Who would have thought that Justine Moritz could have done anything so horrible? She was always so gentle and fond of the family.'

I was horrified. 'Justine Moritz!' I cried. 'It's a mistake. I don't believe it!'

My father shook his head sadly. 'We have proof,' he said. 'She is to be tried later today.'

He told me that Justine had become very ill soon after the murder. She had been forced to stay in bed for several days. During this time, one of the servants happened to move the dress the girl had worn on the night of the murder. As she did so, the locket that William had worn around his neck fell out. It seemed she had murdered the boy in order to rob him.

Just as my father finished this story, Elizabeth entered the room. She had grown into a woman since I had last seen her. She greeted me with the greatest affection. She was very beautiful.

'I've just told Victor about Justine,' said father.

Elizabeth burst into tears. 'It's a disgrace!' she said. 'That girl is innocent. The people in this town hate her as if she were a witch. Nobody will say a good word about her. In my heart, I know that she did not do that terrible thing.'

Tears came into my eyes, but I remained silent. What could I say? I could not tell her about the monster. She would not believe me. Nobody would believe me. They would lock me away in a madhouse. There was nothing I could do to save that poor girl.

My father patted Elizabeth's hand. 'If the girl is innocent,' he said. 'She will be found not guilty at the trial.'

These words calmed me. In my own mind I knew Justine was innocent. I was sure that no jury would hang an innocent woman. All the same, I was sick with worry.

7 The Trial of Justine

At the trial Justine was very calm. She looked over towards my family and tears seemed to fill her eyes. She was beautiful but all the people watching hated her.

Justine explained what had happened on the night of the murder. She told the court that she had spent that day with an aunt. On her way back to my family she had met a man. He had told her that a young boy named William had been lost. She had spent several hours looking for him and when she tried to enter the town of Geneva the gates had been shut. She had spent the night in a barn. Next morning a peasant woman had found her wandering about the very place where the child had been murdered. Later, she was shown the body of William and had become hysterical. She said that she knew it looked suspicious, but she was innocent.

She could not explain how the locket had come to be found in her dress. She could not understand why the murderer might put it there. She did not know why anybody should want to destroy her.

She looked at the jury. 'I am innocent,' she said, 'as God is my witness.' Then she wept.

Several witnesses were called upon to speak. They were people who had known her for many years. But they were frightened to say anything nice about Justine because they saw that everyone hated her.

Elizabeth was furious when she saw this and demanded to speak. 'I am the cousin of the murdered child,' she said, 'but I cannot stand by and watch this girl die just because her so-called friends are cowards. I have known Justine Moritz a long time. She is a kind and gentle girl who loved the dead child deeply. I cannot believe that she killed him. Why on earth should she have wanted to steal that locket? It is not very valuable. If she had wanted it, I would have given it to her gladly. That is how much I respect her.'

The spectators clapped when they heard Elizabeth's speech. They admired her kindness and generosity. But they continued to hate Justine. They still thought she was a murderess. They were disgusted that the girl should be so ungrateful. They wanted her to be hanged, and they shouted out with anger.

That night I could not sleep. I knew Justine was innocent. Had the demon killed my brother and then found a way of destroying this innocent girl?

Next morning I rushed to the court room. My lips and throat were as dry as dust. The jury had come to a decision. Justine had been found guilty and was to be hanged! Elizabeth came to meet me. 'Justine has confessed to the crime,' she said. 'I will never again believe in human goodness.'

Confessed! I could not believe it! Had I not seen the demon with my own eyes? I took Elizabeth by the hand. 'Listen,' I said, 'there is some mistake. We must go and see the poor girl this very moment.'

8　In the Death Cell

We entered the gloomy prison cell. Justine was sitting on some straw at the far end. There were chains around her wrists. These chains were also fixed to the wall. I was horrified and disgusted. They were treating her as if she were a wild animal. And tomorrow she would be hanged by the neck until she was dead.

When she saw us, she fell to her knees and wept. Elizabeth began to cry as well.

'Oh, Justine!' she said. 'Why did you do it? I was so sure that you were innocent. Why did you kill that poor little child?'

'Do you really believe I killed him?' cried Justine. 'Are you going to join my enemies and see me crushed in body and soul?' Her voice was choked with sobs.

Elizabeth was shocked. 'Why did you confess?' she asked. 'The judges might not have condemned you to death if you had not done so.'

'I did confess,' wept Justine, 'but I confessed a lie. Ever since I was put in this prison, the priest has tormented me. He bullied and threatened me. He told me I was a monster. He made me so confused I almost believed him. He said that I must confess otherwise he would see that I was roasted forever in the fires of hell! What could I do? I had no friends. I was sick with a fever. I told a lie. I confessed. And now I am the most miserable creature on God's earth.'

Elizabeth began to weep. She begged forgiveness of Justine for ever thinking her capable of the murder. She said she would speak to the judges. She would try to melt their stony hearts with her tears and her prayers.

Justine shook her head. 'I am not afraid of death any longer,' she said. 'God will give me courage. I leave a sad and bitter world. Perhaps one day I will meet poor William in heaven!'

I walked over to a far corner of the prison. I did not want anybody to see my face. I ground my teeth together and uttered a terrible groan. This poor girl was going to die. I could do nothing to help her. I was the true murderer. It was all my fault. A worm was eating away at the centre of my heart. The flames of hell were burning inside my head and nothing would ever put them out.

We stayed with Justine for several hours. We did all we could to comfort the poor girl. In the end Elizabeth almost had to be dragged away. 'I wish I were to die with you,' she cried. 'I cannot live in this world of misery.'

Justine tried to be cheerful for the sake of Elizabeth. She brushed away her bitter tears and spoke in a gentle voice. 'Goodbye, Elizabeth, my one and only friend. May heaven bless you. I pray to God that this is the last time you are ever made to suffer. Live and be happy, and bring happiness to others.'

Justine was hanged the very next day. Elizabeth's tears could not soften the hearts of the judges and all my words failed to make them change their mind. Justine had died and I had killed her!

Later I was to see my father and Elizabeth shed tears upon the graves of William and Justine. These were the first victims of my evil experiments.

9 Return of the Demon

I began to avoid people. I would row into the middle of the lake and let the boat drift for hours. The only sounds I heard were those of a bat or the frogs by the shore. At times I wanted to jump into the silent lake and end it all. But then I thought of Elizabeth and my father. I had to remain alive. I had to protect them from the evil of the monster. I knew in my heart that the demon would strike again. How I hated that creature! I wanted to take him to the top of the highest mountain and throw him to his death.

Our house was filled with sadness. My father was very ill and poor Elizabeth was beginning to have nightmares. She kept dreaming of monsters thirsting for each other's blood. She felt she was walking along the edges of a pit and thousands of people were crowding around her. In her dream, they kept trying to push her into the pit. She kept seeing herself falling downwards to her death.

One day, I went for a walk into the alps. I wanted to forget my sorrows. I climbed higher and higher. I saw rivers and fields and ruined castles hanging on the edges of steep, pine-covered cliffs. Far above me were the snow-capped peaks of the alps. They were so beautiful! They seemed to belong to another world. They seemed to be a part of a world filled with mighty gods. I watched as avalanches of ice and snow fell downwards with a great rumbling sound. Huge rocks and pine trees, broken like matchsticks, were swept along and fell with a crash into some deep valley.

I walked up dangerous, slippery pathways. I saw mists and clouds and fields of ice. I had never climbed so high in my life. I had never seen such beauty. I took a deep breath and shouted out with joy and triumph.

As I did so, I suddenly saw the figure of a man. It was some distance away. It was coming towards me with superhuman speed. He jumped over huge cracks in the ice and climbed over great rocks as if they were stepping stones. He was much taller than any human being. I could not move. A mist came over my eyes and I felt faint. But the cold air of the mountains quickly brought me back to my senses. I saw the shape more clearly now. It was the demon. It was the monster that I had created! I trembled with rage and horror, I waited for him to come. I was going to fight him to the death!

The creature came near. His face was filled with pain and anger. It was a face almost too horrible for human eyes to look upon. 'Devil!' I shouted. 'Do you dare to come near me? Don't you fear my revenge? Come closer, you horrible creature so that I can trample you into the dust. If only your death could bring those you murdered back to life!'

The demon stopped. Then he spoke. His voice was deep and clear, but somehow sounded more like that of an animal than a human being. 'Look at me, Frankenstein,' he said. 'I am the ugliest of all living things! I am hated by all men. You must help me. If you do not, I will kill and destroy wherever I go. I will spill the life blood of all those you love. None will escape me.'

'You monster!' I yelled. 'The tortures of hell are too good for you. Yes, I created you. Now I must destroy you!'

My anger gave me tremendous strength. I sprang on him. I wanted to tear him to pieces, but he was too quick for me. It was like trying to catch a shadow.

'Stop!' he said. 'You must hear what I have to say. I am far stronger than you. I could easily kill you, but I will spare your life. I am your creature. You gave me life. You are my God. You should treat me with kindness and understanding. Instead, you have treated me as if I were the Devil. You have made my life a living hell. Everywhere I go, I see a happiness I cannot share. I was once kind and good. But misery made me bitter and evil. Frankenstein, you must make me happy. Then I shall once again be kind and good.'

'No!' I yelled. 'I will not listen to you. We are enemies. We must fight to the death.'

Again I tried to catch him, but again he escaped.

'Will you not listen to me?' he snarled. 'Believe me, Frankenstein. I was once kind and good. My soul glowed with love and friendship. But the world did not want my love. I am hated! I am hated by all men. Everywhere I go I am hated. I am forced to live in these deserted mountains. I am forced to sleep in caves of ice. Man is now my enemy. I will make him as miserable as myself. I will destroy thousands. I will become a whirlwind of rage. Only you can save them. Listen to my story, Frankenstein. You must let me speak in my own defence. You accused me of murder, yet you want to murder me. You would murder the creature to whom you gave life. You would have no feelings of pity for me at all.'

I covered my eyes with my hands. 'I curse the day I created you. Go away! I never want to see you again.'

'Come with me,' insisted the demon. 'My story is long and strange. Come to the hut up on the mountains. The sun is still high in the sky. Before it sets behind those cliffs of snow and lights up another part of this earth, you will have heard me. With your help I could lead a harmless life. Otherwise I will become a bloodthirsty killer. I will destroy all those you love.'

As he spoke, he led the way across the ice. I followed. My heart was filled with misery and fear. But I was curious. I wanted to hear his story. I wanted to find out whether or not he had killed my brother. Also, I was beginning to feel responsible for this creature. Should I try to help him? Was it my fault he was so wicked?

We crossed the ice and climbed up a huge rock. The air was cold and the rain began to fall. We entered the hut. The demon was full of hope and I was thoroughly depressed. But I agreed to listen to him. My revolting companion lit a fire. I sat down beside it.

The monster began his story.

10   The Monster's First Experiences

I find it difficult to remember the first few weeks of my life. Everything was misty and confused. I could see, hear, feel and smell. I kept falling down. My eyes hurt. I could only see vague shapes. The heat began to worry me. I wandered off into a forest and lay down by the side of a stream. I rested. Then I was tormented by hunger and thirst. I ate some berries which I found hanging on the trees or lying on the ground. I drank from the stream. Soon I fell asleep.

It was dark when I awoke. I felt cold and frightened. I was all alone in a strange world. I had put on some clothes before leaving your house, but these did not protect me from the damp of the night. I was helpless and miserable. I sat down and wept.

Soon a gentle light came into the sky and filled me with pleasure. I stood up and watched a shining circle rise from among the trees. I stared with a kind of wonder. It moved slowly, but it lit up my path and I set off in search of berries. There were no clear ideas in my mind. Everything was still confused. I felt light and hunger and thirst and darkness. Hundreds of sounds rang in my ears. Smells of all kinds came to my nostrils. I saw the bright moon shining in the sky.

Several days passed. I began to see things more clearly. I could see the clear stream which gave me drink and the trees which shaded me with their leaves. Then I heard the sweet sounds of song. These came from the throats of the little winged animals who kept fluttering about in front of my eyes. Sometimes I tried to imitate the pleasant song of these creatures, but I was not able to do so. Strange grunting noises came from my mouth and I was frightened.

My eyes became better and better. I could now see insects and flowers. I learned that the sparrow could only make a harsh sound but the blackbird's song was sweet and musical.

One day I found a fire which had been left by wandering beggars. I was overcome with delight at the warmth it gave out. In my joy I thrust my hands into the live embers. The next moment I pulled them out again with a cry of pain. This I could not understand. But I learned to heap wood upon the fire to keep it going. Then I found some of the scraps and leftovers that the beggars had roasted. They tasted delicious.

But food became scarce. I often spent the whole day looking for a few nuts to satisfy my hunger. I had to leave that place. I set off across the wood towards the setting sun. Three days passed and at length I discovered the open country. There had been a great fall of snow the night before and the fields were a clear white. This filled me with sadness and I found my feet chilled by the cold damp substance that covered the ground.

It was about seven o'clock in the morning and I longed to find food and shelter. At last I saw a small hut which had been built for a shepherd. This was a new sight and I looked at it with great curiosity.

The door was open, so I entered.

11   The Monster Meets Man

There was an old man inside the hut. He was sitting by the fire eating his breakfast. He turned round on hearing a noise. When he saw me, he gave a loud shriek. His plate fell to the floor with a clatter and he dashed out of the hut. I watched him run across the fields with tremendous speed. I was astonished. What was the matter with him?

I was delighted by the appearance of the hut. Here the snow and rain could not enter. The ground was perfectly dry. I felt I had found myself a home. I greedily ate what was left of the shepherd's breakfast. This consisted of bread, milk, cheese and wine. It was delicious, apart from the wine which I did not like. Then I was so tired, I lay down amongst some straw and went to sleep.

It was noon when I awoke. The sun was warm and shone brightly on the white ground. I decided to go exploring. I put some food into a bag and walked across the fields for hours. By sunset I arrived at a village. How beautiful it was! There were huts, cottages and large expensive houses. I saw vegetables in the gardens. There was milk and cheese in the windows of some of the cottages. I became curious. I entered one of the best of these houses. As I did so, the children screamed and one of the women fainted. The whole village woke up. Some people ran away in terror and some attacked me. I was pelted with sticks and stones and pieces of metal. Huge bruises began to appear on my body. I escaped and ran away across the countryside. I was forced to hide in a small hovel which joined on to a cottage in the middle of some fields. There I remained until the next morning.

This was my first experience of the cruelty of human beings. Why did they hate me so?

12 The Monster Receives an Education

Early next morning I got up and examined my new living place. The hut was four feet high. The walls were filled with small holes and the wind whistled through them. There was a pig sty on one side and a clear pool of water on the other. I blocked up the hole through which I had entered with stones and wood so that none would know that I lived there. Next, I covered the floor with a carpet of straw and began to eat a loaf which I had managed to steal. I was happy. This place was paradise compared to the cold forest with its rain-dropping branches and damp earth.

I was about to remove a plank so I could get some water when I heard a footstep. I looked through a hole in the wall and saw a little girl carrying a pail half-filled with milk. She was then joined by a young man and a young woman who led her into the cottage. I was curious. I moved towards the far wall of my hut. To my delight, there was a crack in the wall and I was able to look directly into the cottage.

I saw a small room. It was whitewashed and clean, but there was hardly any furniture. An old man sat near a fire. He looked very sad. I watched as the little girl went over to a drawer and took out something made of wood. She gave it to the old man and he began to produce sounds sweeter than the song of the thrush or the nightingale. I saw tears appear in the eyes of the girl and her parents. The old man was blind.

I was filled with wonder. I had never seen anything so beautiful in my life. I watched the old man lift up the little girl and kiss her. This action filled my whole body with a mixture of pain and pleasure. I could not explain this. It was a feeling even stronger than cold or hunger, even stronger than my desire for food and warmth.

Night came quickly. To my surprise, the cottagers lit candles and the room was lit up with a strange kind of light.

Once again the old man took up his instrument and began to play. I watched all this in amazement. Then the candles went out and the family, I suppose, went to sleep.

I watched these cottagers for several months and learned many things. I learned how to speak. I went deep into the lonely forest and tried to imitate the sounds made by my cottagers. I wanted to show myself to them and to speak to them. I knew by now I was ugly. I had seen my face in the pool of water beside my hut. I was so unlike the cottagers! I was filled with anger and shame. But there was hope. If I learned to speak like them and if I learned to understand their way of life perhaps they would not be so frightened by my ugliness. Perhaps they could learn to love me.

I learned of the difference between the sexes, and the birth and growth of children. This made me sad. Where were my friends and relations? No father had ever watched me at play. No mother had ever blessed me with smiles and kisses. What was I? I kept asking myself this question again and again. When I looked around, I saw and heard nothing like me. Was I truly a monster? Was this why men ran away from me or pelted me with stones and pieces of wood?

I learned how to read. I listened as the cottagers read to the old man. Then I stole the books and put them back later. The more I read, the more I began to wonder who I was and where I had come from. I read how God had created Adam and wondered who had created me. I read how the Devil had been thrown into hell. I learned that the Devil and all his followers were as ugly as myself. Was I a devil? Was I a monster?

One day, I reached into the pocket of the clothes I had taken from your laboratory. I found some papers. Now that I could read, I looked at them with great excitement. They were the notes you made when you were creating me! Now I knew the truth. I was filled with disgust and anger. 'Cursed be the day that I first received life!' I cried. I was filled with agony. I cursed the name of Frankenstein. Why did you make a monster so ugly that even you turned from me in disgust?

God made man beautiful, but you made me a thing of horror.

But I did not give up hope. The cottagers were so good and kind. Surely they would be able to ignore my horrid and deformed appearance? After all, the poor crippled beggars that stopped by their door were never driven away. In a few months' time I would show myself to them.

I began to think of Paradise. I imagined lovely creatures who would show me love and affection. I saw them smile like angels, and my days were filled with everlasting joy. But it was all a dream. I had no Eve. I had no woman to bring me happiness and comfort. God had given Adam a mate. Where was my god? He had deserted me and I cursed him in my heart.

The months passed by. I was afraid to show myself. I waited until the blind man was all alone. Then I entered the cottage door. My heart was beating madly.

13 The Monster Shows Himself to the Cottagers

All was silent in the cottage. I knocked.

'Who is there?' said the old man. 'Please come in.'

I entered. 'I am sorry to disturb you,' I said. 'I am a traveller and I am very tired. Could I possibly stay for a few minutes by your fire?'

'Come in,' said the old man. 'I will do what I can to help you, but I am blind. My children are out in the fields and I shall find it difficult to get you any food.'

'There is no need to worry,' I replied. 'I have some food. It is only warmth and rest that I need.'

I sat down and there was silence. I knew that every minute was precious but I did not know how to begin the conversation.

The old man spoke. 'Do you come from these parts?'

'No. I come from Geneva. There are some people I wish to meet. I love them dearly and I hope they will love me.'

'I wish you good luck.'

'These people have never seen me before. They do not know me at all. I am full of fear. If I fail to win their friendship, I will be all alone for the rest of my life.'

'Do not despair. It is terrible to have no friends, but the hearts of men are full of love. Be hopeful.'

'These people are the most excellent creatures in the world. However, they are prejudiced against me. I am good. I have never harmed anybody. I have feelings and I am kind, but when they look upon me they will only see me as a terrible monster.'

'That is very unfortunate. But if you are free from any sin, can't you make them believe in your goodness?'

'That is what I am about to do. That is why I am so afraid. I love these friends with all my heart, but they believe I wish to hurt them. It is this prejudice that I must overcome.'

'Where do these friends live?'

'Very near this spot.'

The old man was silent for a moment. Then he spoke. 'If you give me all the details of your story, perhaps I could convince them of your goodness. I am blind and I cannot see your face, but I believe you to be sincere. I would be happy to help a fellow human being.'

'Bless you! I accept your generous offer. You have lifted me up from the dust. I hope that with your help I will not be driven away from human society like a wild and dangerous animal.'

'God forbid!' cried the old man. 'That should never happen, not even to a criminal. Such treatment makes men evil and desperate. It is a shocking thing to do to a fellow human being.'

'How can I ever thank you? I have never heard such kindness from the lips of men before.'

'Could you tell me the names of these friends and where they live?'

I was silent for a moment. This was the most important moment of my short life. I would either be happy or miserable forever. I tried to speak but the effort was too much for me. I sat down in a chair and sobbed loudly.

At that moment I heard the footsteps of the rest of the family. I did not have a moment to lose. I grabbed the hand of the old man. I cried, 'Save and protect me! You and your family are the friends I was talking about. Do not fail me in my hour of greatest need!'

'Great God!' exclaimed the old man. 'Who are you?'

At that moment the cottage door opened. The rest of the family entered. Who can describe their horror and amazement on seeing me? The little girl fainted and the woman ran out of the cottage screaming. The man rushed forward and with the strength of ten men he tore me from his father to whose knees I was clinging. In a fit of rage and hate, he threw me to the ground. Then he struck me violently with a stick. I could have torn him into little pieces just as the lion rips

apart the antelope. But my heart was filled with sickness and disappointment and I did nothing. He lifted up his stick to strike me a second time. I dodged the blow and ran out through the door. Nobody saw me escape into the safety of my hut.

14 The Monster Becomes Filled with Hate 憎恨

I cursed you, Frankenstein. I cursed you from the bottom of my heart. I wanted to kill myself. I wanted to kill you. I wanted revenge. I could have destroyed the cottage in my hate. I could have torn the cottagers to pieces. I would have enjoyed listening to their screams and their misery. It would have been like a feast.

When night came, I left my hut and wandered into the wood. There I began to shriek and howl. I was like a wild beast that had broken out of its cage. I raced through the forest with the speed of a stag. I tore up trees and destroyed everything that got in my way.

That night was filled with misery. The cold stars seemed to laugh at me. The bare trees waved their branches above me. Now and then the sweet voice of a bird echoed in the silence. All creatures except me were asleep or happy. I was as miserable as the devil. I felt as if I were trapped forever in the burning fires of hell. I wanted to destroy the world. I wanted to crush it in the palm of my fist or to choke it with my bare hands.

In despair and exhaustion, I fell asleep.

Next morning the sun rose. I felt refreshed. I realized I had acted like a fool. I should not have shown myself to the rest of the family. I should have had spent more time explaining to the old man that I was so terribly ugly to look at. Perhaps it was not too late. I decided to return to the cottage and try once more to win the old man's friendship.

These thoughts made me feel calmer. In the afternoon I fell into a deep sleep. But the fever in my blood did not allow me to enjoy pleasant dreams. I kept seeing the little girl fainting. I kept seeing the woman running from the cottage screaming like a lunatic. And I saw the man tearing me from his father's feet and beating me with a stick. I woke up exhausted and found that night had already fallen. I crept from my hiding place and went back to the hut.

The sun rose once more. I waited for the family to get up, but all was silent. I bit my lips and trembled. Where were they?

Presently the husband came into the cottage with the landlord. I listened carefully to their words.

'Do you know what you are doing?' said the landlord. 'You will lose three months rent and all the vegetables in the garden. Wouldn't it be better to wait for a few days and think it over?'

'No,' said the cottager, shaking his head. 'We will never again live in your cottage. The place is haunted by a demon. My father will soon die as a result of shock and my wife and child will never recover from their horror.'

The man shuddered violently as he said this. The two men spent a few minutes picking up their belongings and then left. I never saw the cottagers again.

I spent the rest of the day in the hut. I was filled with despair. I had been deserted. There was now no hope of ever being loved.

My feelings of self-pity gave way to those of hatred. I destroyed all the vegetables in the garden and began to heap wood and straw around the hut. The moon rose out of the sky and a fierce wind came out of the woods. The clouds were swept from the sky. The blast was like a mighty avalanche and my mind was filled with a terrible madness. I lit the dry branch of a tree and danced with fury around the cottage. I waved this torch about my head and with a wild scream I set fire to the wood and straw. The wind fanned the fire and the cottage was quickly covered with flames. I watched these flames cling to the building and lick at it with their snake-like tongues.

I was now a creature of evil. I decided to come looking for you, my dear Frankenstein. You were the man who had created me. You were the man who had made me into this frightful monster.

15　The Monster's Good Deed

It was a long journey to Geneva. I travelled only at night. I was out in the open the whole time and it was bitterly cold. Rain and snow poured around me. Mighty rivers were frozen. The surface of the earth was hard and bare.

But as I came nearer to Switzerland, the sun became warmer and the land turned to green. One morning, I found that my path lay through a deep wood. I decided to travel on during the daylight. It was spring. The weather was so beautiful that even I felt cheerful.

As I came out of the woods, I saw a deep and fast-flowing river. The trees were all around and bent their branches into it. Suddenly I heard the sound of voices. I hid behind some bushes and waited. A young girl came running towards the spot where I lay hidden. She was playing hide and seek with somebody. I watched as she ran along the steep bank of the river. Suddenly she slipped and fell into the stream.

Without thinking, I rushed from my hiding-place. I dived into the waters and caught hold of her. The current was fast and I had great difficulty in dragging her to the shore. The girl was unconscious. She lay upon the grass and did not move. I tried very hard to bring her back to life. As I did so, a farmer appeared. He ran towards me and tore the girl from my arms. Then he raced away into the deeper part of the woods. I followed him. He turned round and aimed a gun at me. He fired and I fell to the ground.

I watched the man disappear and I clenched my fists with rage. Was this the reward for my kind action? I began to twist about on the ground. I was in pain. Part of my flesh and bone had been shattered. All my feelings of gentleness gave way to hellish fury. I ground my teeth and snarled like a wild animal. I was determined to hate the human race for the rest of my life. But the agony of my wound was too great for me. I fainted.

For some weeks after, I led a miserable life in the woods. I tried to cure my wound. The bullet had entered my shoulder and I could not get it out. I promised that one day I would be revenged upon my enemies.

When my wound had healed, I continued my journey. Soon I arrived outside the town of Geneva. It was here that I fell asleep.

Little did I know that my revenge was soon to come.

報復

① A farmer fired him and he was hurt

16   The Monster's Revenge

I was woken up by the approach of a beautiful child. He came running towards the place where I had hidden. He was full of life and energy. As I watched him, an idea came into my head. The child seemed far too young to know anything about the horror of my deformed body. I decided to capture him. I would teach him to become my friend and companion just as a man teaches a dog to love and respect him.

With this in mind, I grabbed him as he went past. The moment he saw me, he placed his hands before his eyes and uttered a shrill scream. I dragged his hands away from his face. 'Do not scream,' I said. 'I don't wish to hurt you. Listen to me.'

He struggled violently. 'Let me go,' he cried. 'Monster! Ugly beast! You wish to eat me and tear me to pieces. Let me go or I will tell my father.'

'Boy,' I said, 'you will never see your father again. You must come with me.'

'Monster! Let me go. My father is a very important man. He is Mr Frankenstein. He will catch and punish you. You had better let me go.'

'Frankenstein!' I snarled. 'Then you are a relative of my hated enemy. You will be my first victim.'

The child continued to struggle. He kept on calling me names and insulting me. My heart was filled with despair and anger. I squeezed his throat to silence him. In a moment he lay dead at my feet.

I looked down on my victim. His neck and face had turned blue and his tongue hung from his mouth. My heart swelled with joy and triumph. I clapped my hands. I shouted out, 'I too can cause suffering and death. It is the turn of my enemy to feel pain. I will be revenged. The life of Frankenstein will not be worth living.' As I fixed my eyes on the child, I saw something glittering on his chest. I took it. It was a portrait of a most lovely woman. For a few moments I gazed with delight on her dark eyes and her lovely lips. But presently my rage returned. I remembered that such a creature could never love me. If she ever saw me, she would scream or her face would become ugly with disgust and fear. At that moment, I wanted to rush upon the town and tear every living person to pieces.

Suddenly I felt tired. I needed rest. I left the spot where the murder had been committed and looked for a better hiding-place. I entered a barn, thinking it was empty. Inside, I saw a woman sleeping on some straw. She was young and beautiful. I wondered if she could ever love me. I bent over her and whispered, 'Awake, my beauty. Your lover is near. I would give up my life if you would just give me one kiss.'

She stirred in her sleep. A thrill of terror ran through my body. Would she wake up? Would she curse me? Would she afterwards find the dead child and let the world know that I was a murderer? But she did not wake. A hellish idea came into my mind. I decided that she would be punished for my crime. I bent over her and placed the portrait in one of the pockets of her dress. She moved again and I ran away.

For some days I haunted the spot where the murder had taken place. Sometimes I wanted to see you and sometimes I wanted to kill myself and put an end to all my sufferings for ever. At length I wandered towards these mountains. I have travelled all through their deep valleys. I was filled with a burning wish that only you can do something about. You will never be rid of me until you have given me this help. I am alone and I am miserable. You must make me a woman who is as deformed and ugly as myself! She alone will not run away from me in terror. She will be my companion and my wife! You must do this for me, I am your creature and you must help me!'

17   The Promise

The monster stopped speaking and looked at me. He was waiting for a reply.

'I refuse,' I said. 'And no torture in hell shall ever make me change my mind. I shall never create another creature like yourself. The two of you together might destroy the world with your wickedness.'

'Listen to me,' replied the demon. 'I am only wicked because I am unhappy. If you had your way, you would throw me off a cliff into a valley of ice and you would not call this murder. Why should I pity my victims if they don't pity me? If you don't help me, I will destroy everyone who comes within my reach. I will do everything in my power to make you miserable. I will make you wish you had never been born.'

The demon trembled as he spoke. He was filled with a horrible rage and his face twisted into all sorts of frightful shapes. But he calmed himself and continued speaking. 'You are the cause of my sufferings and my crimes. I am not asking for too much. My demands are quite reasonable. All I want is a woman who is as ugly and deformed as myself. I know we will be monsters. I know we will be cut off from the world. That will not bother us. We will be happy with one another. We will lead a harmless and happy life. Have pity on me, Frankenstein! Don't refuse me!'

I took a deep breath. I was beginning to feel sorry for the monster I had so foolishly created. He was intelligent and sensitive. He had all the feelings of a normal human being. Should I try to make him happy?

The demon saw my change of mood and continued. He was very persuasive. 'If you agree to do this,' he said, 'neither you nor any other human being will ever see me again. I will go into the vast jungles of South America. I do not eat the

same food as man. I do not have to kill sheep or cattle to fill
my stomach. I can live off nuts and berries. My companion
will do the same. We shall make our bed of dry leaves. The
sun will shine upon us and ripen our food. We shall live a life
of peace.'

'How can I be sure?' I said. 'You may return to the world
of men. You may try to win their kindness and their love.
Once again they will hate you and try to destroy you. Then
you will become angry again. And you will have a companion
who will help you to murder all who stand in your way.'

The monster gave a groan. 'Now you are torturing me,' he
said. 'Why should I return to the world of men? I will live in
complete happiness with my wife. Why should I return to
those who hate me?'

His words had a strange effect on me. I felt sorry for him. I
even wanted to comfort him. But when I looked at that
filthy mass that walked and talked, I felt sick. My feelings
would change to horror and hatred. This made me feel guilty.
It was my fault that he was so ugly. I had no right to prevent
him from being happy.

'You promise you will be harmless,' I said, 'but how can I
trust you? Perhaps this is just a trick. Perhaps you just want
more power so that your revenge can be all the more terrible.'

'You must trust me,' he said. 'If I have a companion, I will
bless my maker. I will be at peace with mankind. I will once
again become kind and gentle. If I am to remain alone, I will
get worse and worse. I will make the world suffer. I will make
the world as miserable as myself.'

I said nothing. I was thinking. Perhaps the monster would
become kind and good if he had a companion. If I did not
agree to help him, he might well become a murdering
madman. He could live in caves of ice. He could climb huge
mountains as if they were tiny hills. Nobody would be able
to catch him or track him down. He could raid towns and
villages and murder whenever he wished. I decided that it
would be better to help this creature.

'I agree to help you,' I said, 'on one condition. You must

swear to leave Europe forever. You must swear to leave every place inhabited by man. If you agree to do this, I will give you a female who will go with you.'

'I swear by the sun and the blue skies of heaven,' he cried. 'If you make me this female, you will never see my face again. Now you must go home and begin your work. I shall keep a check on your progress. When you are ready, I shall appear.'

Then he left me. I saw him go down the mountain faster than an eagle in full flight. He disappeared amongst the hills of ice.

His story had lasted the whole day. The sun would soon fall below the mountains. I began to walk down towards the village. But my heart was heavy and my steps were slow. All the time I kept thinking about the promise I had made to the monster. My mind kept swirling about like a whirlpool. It was already night when I arrived at a resting place.

I sat down beside a fountain. Every so often the clouds were swept away and the stars shone down upon me. The dark pine trees were all around. Here and there a broken branch lay on the ground. It was so strange and quiet. I wanted to stay in that spot forever. I wanted to disappear from the face of the earth. I wanted to be swept away by a blast of wind.

Then morning came. I went down to a nearby village but I did not rest there. I went straight to Geneva. I felt as if the weight of the mountains were pressing down upon me. I was in agony. I returned home and showed myself to the family. They were horrified by the wildness of my appearance. But I would not answer their questions. I was ashamed. I did not feel worthy to speak to them. Yet I loved them. I had to save them. That was why I was going to set about my dreadful work. But I was worried. Was I doing the right thing? That question kept repeating itself again and again inside my brain. Was I doing the right thing?

18 Frankenstein Travels to England

But I was not able to begin the work. Days and weeks passed by. I feared the revenge of the disappointed demon, but I did not have the courage to start on that dreadful task. I spent whole days all alone in a small boat in the middle of the lake. I watched the clouds and listened to the rippling of the waves. It was almost as if I had been hypnotized.

It was then that my father told me that I should marry Elizabeth. He was an old man and did not want to die before this happy event. I loved Elizabeth with all my heart but I did not want to marry her straight away. I had to create a female for the monster first. If I did not, he would seek his revenge. I told my father I would marry Elizabeth when I arrived back from England. I wanted to go to that country to obtain information which would help me in my experiments. Also, I knew the monster would follow me and my family would therefore be safe from his cruelty.

I left Switzerland in September. I was very sad to say goodbye to Elizabeth. Two days later I arrived in Strasbourg. It was here that I met Henry Clerval again. Father had asked him to accompany me on my long journey. What a contrast there was between us! He was so happy and full of life, and I was so depressed.

We took a boat and sailed down the Rhine through Germany. The scenery was very beautiful. We saw islands surrounded by willow trees and many picturesque towns. There were black woods and vineyards with green sloping banks. I lay down in the bottom of the boat and stared upwards at the blue sky. I could hear the song of workers as we glided down the stream. Henry was overjoyed. He felt as if he had been carried away into a fairyland.

'I have seen so many beautiful sights in my own country,' he said. 'I have been to the lakes where the snowy mountains seem to fall into the waters. I have seen these lakes shaken by storms. I have seen the storm tear up whirlwinds of water. I have stood on the spot where a priest and his dog were carried away by an avalanche of snow and listened to the cry of their dying voices in the wind. I have seen all these things, Victor, but nothing can compare with the charm of this land. When you see such beauty you know that there is a God in heaven.'

Poor Clerval! Where are you now? Your body lies beneath the soil and the worms eat away at your flesh. Are you in heaven? Your beauty has withered and rotted like the leaves in autumn. I pray to God that your soul is watching over me!

Please excuse my sorrow. Henry is now dead and I simply had to tell the world of his goodness. I will now continue with my story.

At Cologne we left our boat and travelled by carriage to Rotterdam. Then we journeyed by ship to England. Suddenly my heart was filled with sadness and fear. I had not forgotten the task I had to do. I had not forgotten my promise to the monster. And he had not forgotten me.

We spent four weeks in London. I visited the English scientists and obtained all the information I needed. Then I began to collect together all the materials I required for my experiments. I did this in secret. I did not want Henry to become involved in the horrors of my work.

I received a letter from Scotland. It came from a friend who had once spent some time with my family in Geneva. He wanted me to visit him in Perth. I accepted this invitation as it fitted in with my plans. I told Clerval I wanted to make the tour of Scotland on my own. I was worried that he might be harmed by the demon.

Once I had left my friend I set off on my journey. I did not go to Perth. I went to the Orkneys. Here I would find a lonely place where no one would disturb my work.

At last I found such an island. I rented a miserable-looking hut. The roof had fallen in and the door had come off its hinges. I had it repaired and converted it into a place which would be suitable for my experiments.

Each day my work became more and more horrible. Sometimes I could not bear to enter my laboratory for several days. At other times I slaved day and night in order to complete my work. It was a filthy kind of work. When I had first made the monster I had been excited and full of hope. I had not been too bothered by the horror of what I was doing. Now that I was working in cold blood, I was filled with disgust. My heart was made sick by the work of my hands.

The scenery of the island made me feel nervous. The beach was covered with rocks and stones of various sizes. The waves of the sea roared and crashed against my feet. It was a very monotonous scene. The land was bare and the cattle looked half-starved. I kept thinking of the beauty of Switzerland with its hills covered with vines and cottages. How different it was from this terrible place! Here the giant ocean roars all day and all night like a spirit from the land of the dead.

As I worked, I was filled with fear. I kept imagining that the demon was watching me all the time. I was sick in my heart and I kept asking myself the same question: Am I doing the right thing? Am I doing the right thing?

Bit by bit, the creature in the laboratory was taking shape.

19　Curse of the Demon

I sat one evening in my laboratory. I was alone. The sun had just set and the moon was rising from the sea. There was not enough light for my work. I was beginning to have second thoughts about the promise I had made. Three years ago I had produced a creature who had turned into a murdering monster. This creature had brought misery to those I loved and had filled my heart with sorrow. I was now about to make another such creature. I had no way of knowing how she would behave. She might become ten thousand times more evil than her mate. She might delight in murder for its own sake. She might enjoy torturing people and causing them misery. The demon had sworn to leave the civilized world and hide himself in deserts and jungles where no one might see his face. But she had made no such promise. She might refuse to go with him. The two creatures might even hate each other. The demon was disgusted by his own ugliness. He might be even more disgusted by the sight of the female I had created for him. And she might turn in disgust from him. She might be attracted by the superior beauty of man. Then the demon would become even more cruel.

Even if they liked one another and went into the jungles of South America there would still be problems. Supposing they had children? They might produce a race of devils who would conquer the world and destroy mankind or turn them into terrified slaves. The name of Frankenstein would be cursed forever.

I then looked up and my heart almost stopped beating. In the light of the moon I could see the demon. He was standing by the window. A terrible grin wrinkled his lips. Yes, he had followed me on my travels. He had walked through forests, he had hidden himself in caves. He had watched me all the time.

His face was filled with treachery and cunning. I knew he could not be trusted. I knew I had made a terrible mistake! I trembled with fear and anger. I began to tear the creature to pieces with my bare hands. Soon they became covered with blood and pieces of muscle. My fingernails were choked with skin and hair. I almost fainted with disgust and horror.

The demon gave a loud howl of despair and disappeared from the window.

I left the room and locked the door. I made a promise in my own heart that I would never again begin that work. Then with shaking steps I went back to my own room. I was alone. There was nobody to help or comfort me.

Several hours passed. I remained at my window gazing at the sea. It seemed almost motionless. The winds made no noise and all nature seemed to be resting under the quiet eye of the moon. A few fishing boats were on the water and I sometimes heard the sound of voices as the fishermen called to one another. Then I heard the paddling of oars near the shore. Someone had landed close to my house.

In a few minutes I heard the creaking of my door. I trembled from head to foot. I wanted to shout out to one of the peasants who lived in a cottage not too far away. I was not able to do this. I was frozen to the spot. I was like a child who wants to run away from a nightmare, but finds he cannot move.

Presently I heard the sound of footsteps along the passage. The door opened and the demon appeared. He closed the door behind him. Then he came near me. He was snarling with rage. 'You have destroyed the work which you began,' he said. 'What are you trying to do? Do you dare to break your promise? I have suffered great hardships because of you. I left Switzerland with you. I crept along the shores of the Rhine. I was there amongst its islands of willow and I climbed over the tops of its hills. I have lived many weeks in the moors of England and among the deserts of Scotland. I have suffered cold and hunger. You cannot imagine how I have suffered. Do you dare destroy my hopes?'

'Yes. I am breaking my promise. I will never create another monster such as you. I now see you for what you really are, a creature of evil!'

'You slave!' roared the demon. 'I can make your life a living hell. You are my creator, but I am your master. You will obey me!'

'Never!' I shouted. 'Your threats are useless. Do you really think I will create another monster such as yourself?'

The monster saw the determination in my face. He gnashed his teeth together in anger. 'Each man has a wife and each beast has a mate,' he snarled. 'Why must I be all alone? Do you think I will allow others to be happy while I am miserable? I will have my revenge. I will wait and I will watch you with the cunning of a serpent. Beware my sting!'

'Do your worst, you spiteful demon! I will never change my mind.'

'Very well,' he said. 'I will go. But remember this: I will be with you on your wedding night!'

I moved forward and tried to catch him. But he was far too quick for me. He raced out of the house with the speed of lightning. A few moments later, he was in his boat. It flew across the waters like an arrow. Soon it was lost amongst the waves.

All was again silent. But his words still rang in my ears. I was burning with rage. I wanted to follow this demon and throw him to the bottom of the ocean. I walked up and down in my room. I was very worried. A thousand terrible nightmares rushed through my mind. I shuddered. Who would be his next victim? Then I remembered his words, 'I will be with you on your wedding night!' That would be the date of my death. The demon would strike and his revenge would be ended. I was not afraid. Death would be a release from my misery. What angered and upset me was the suffering that would be caused to Elizabeth when her husband was snatched away from her on the wedding night. No doubt that was all part of the demon's plan of revenge. I clenched my fists in fury. Let the demon come, I said to myself. When he comes I will be ready for him!

20 Burial at Sea

The night passed away and the sun rose from the ocean. I felt
calmer. I left the house and walked on the beach. I wanted to
stay on this island forever. If I returned to Geneva, I would
be killed. I would see those I loved die in the grasp of the
demon. To think that I had created this monster with my
own hands!

I walked about the island like a restless ghost. I was lonely
and miserable. The sun rose higher in the sky and I became
sleepy. I had been awake the whole night and my eyes were
red and sore. I lay down on the grass and fell into a deep
sleep.

When I awoke, I felt refreshed. Yet the words of the
demon still rang in my ears like a death bell.

The sun was beginning to set. I was starving. I sat down
and started to eat an oat cake. It was then I saw a fishing
boat. It landed close to me and one of the men brought me
a packet. It contained letters from Geneva and one from
Clerval. My friend wrote that he had to go back to London
soon and he wanted to see me as quickly as possible. He was
waiting for me in Perth. I decided I would leave the island
and join him in two days time.

But before I departed I had a job to do. I shuddered at the
thought of doing it. I had to pack up my chemical instruments. I had to collect them from that room. The next
morning I plucked up enough courage to open the door of
the laboratory. The remains of the half-finished creature lay _into sea_
scattered upon the floor. I almost felt as if I had mangled the
living flesh of a human being. I packed up my instruments.
Then I put all the pieces of the body into a basket and filled
it up with heavy stones. I had decided to throw them into the
sea that very night. I did not want the local peasants to
become suspicious and horrified by all those pieces of

mangled flesh and bone.

Between two and three in the morning, the moon rose in the sky. I put my basket into a little boat and sailed four miles from the shore. The sea was almost empty. There were only one or two boats returning towards land. I sailed away from them. I felt as though I were about to commit a dreadful crime. I wanted to avoid any meetings with my fellow human beings. Suddenly the moon was covered over by a thick cloud. I took advantage of this moment of darkness and threw my basket into the sea. I listened to the gurgling sound as it sank. Then I sailed away from the spot.

As I sailed back to shore, the sky became completely clouded. But the air was pure and sweet. It refreshed me and raised my spirits. I decided to stay on the water a while longer. I fixed the rudder to stop the boat from moving. Then I lay down at the bottom of the boat. Clouds hid the moon. Everything became dark. I could only hear the sound of the waves gently splashing against the boat as it swayed from side to side. The murmur of the water was like music. In no time at all I was sound asleep.

I do not know how long I was asleep. When I woke up I had a shock. The wind had become very strong. Large waves were sweeping all around my little boat. I had been driven far from the coast. I wanted to turn around. I pulled on the rudder. To my dismay, the waves came leaping over the sides of the boat and almost filled it. I had no choice. I had to let the wind carry me forward like a leaf in a storm. I was frightened for my life. I had no compass with me. I did not know where I was going. I might be swept into the wide Atlantic ocean. There I would feel the tortures of starvation. The waves grew larger. They roared and battered the tiny boat. Perhaps I would be swallowed up by these savage waters!

I had already been out for many hours. I began to feel the torment of a burning thirst. I looked up to the heavens. Fast-flying clouds were racing across the sky with incredible speed. I looked upon the sea. Was this to be my grave?

'Devil!' I exclaimed. 'Your revenge has come!' I thought of
Elizabeth, of my father and of Clerval. They would be next
to suffer from the evil cruelty of the monster. I fell into a
daydream of despair and horror.

Hours passed by. The sun began to fall towards the
horizon. The wind died away into a gentle breeze. There were
no more huge waves upon the sea, but the boat kept rocking
from side to side. I felt sick. I was too weak to hold the
rudder properly. Then, all of a sudden, I saw land towards
the south. I was saved!

Tears of joy filled my eyes. Strength came flooding back
into my heart. I tore off my shirt and made it into a sail. I
could now see trees. There were ships near the shore. I saw a
church steeple pointing towards heaven. I sailed into the
harbour. I had escaped the anger of the sea.

A crowd gathered round. They watched me pull down the
sails. They whispered together. Nobody offered to help me. I
looked at them closely. They were frowning. There was
hatred in their eyes.

'My good friends,' I said. 'I am tired and hungry. I have
been lost at sea. Will you tell me the name of this town?'

'You will find out soon enough,' replied a man with a
rough voice. 'We have a little room waiting for you.'

I did not understand this rudeness. 'Why do you answer
me so roughly?' I replied. 'Is it the custom of Englishmen to
be so rude to strangers?'

I do not know about the customs of the English,' snarled
the man. 'This is Ireland. And it is the custom of the Irish to
hate villains.'

The crowd grew quickly. Their faces were full of curiosity
and anger. I was worried and annoyed. I asked if there was a
place in town where I might find food and rest. Nobody
answered. Then I moved forward. The crowd began to
murmur. They followed me and surrounded me. A man came
up to me. He tapped me on the shoulder. 'Come along, sir.
You must follow me to Mr Kirwin.'

'Who is Mr Kirwin?' I said. 'Why should I follow you? Is

this not a free country?'

'Yes sir,' said the man. 'This is a free country for honest people. Mr Kirwin is a judge. You have some explaining to do. Last night a man was murdered here. We found his body by the sea shore.'

At first I was alarmed, but then I grew calmer. I was innocent. This could easily be proved. I followed the man in silence. He took me to one of the best houses in the town. I was so exhausted I almost collapsed. However, I kept on my feet. If I fell down, the crowd would see this as a sign that I was guilty and frightened. I did not realize what was in store for me. I did not know that I was soon to be overwhelmed by horror and despair.

I must pause here. It requires all my strength to tell the rest of this story.

21   A Dreadful Shock

Mr Kirwin was a wise old man. He was pleasant but strict. He asked some witnesses to tell him what had happened the previous night.

I learned that three fishermen had found a dead body on the sand. At first they had thought it was the corpse of a person who had been drowned and washed ashore. Then they had looked more carefully. To their surprise the body was dry and still warm. They had carried it to the cottage of an old woman. There they had tried to bring the body back to life, but they had failed. The corpse was that of a handsome young man. His death had been caused by strangling. On his neck were the black marks of the murderer's fingers.

When I heard about the marks of the fingers, my mouth fell open with shock. I suddenly remembered the murder of my brother. My arms and legs trembled. A mist came over my eyes. I was forced to lean against a chair to stop myself from falling. Mr Kirwin noticed this. No doubt he saw it as a sign of a guilty conscience.

One of the other fishermen had some more information. He said he had seen a man leaving the shore in a boat just before the body was discovered. He said it was the same boat as the one in which I had just landed.

They all claimed that I was the murderer. They said the storm had probably blown my boat back to the shore. That was why I had not been able to make my escape.

Mr Kirwin listened to the evidence. Then he said I should be shown the dead body. He wanted to see what my reaction would be. They took me along to a nearby house. I was not the least bit worried. I had been talking to some peasants in the Orkneys on the night of the murder. What had I to fear?

I entered the room where the corpse lay. Then I was led up to the coffin. The lid was pulled back and I was able to gaze down on the face of the victim.

How can I describe my feelings when I saw him? Even now my throat is as dry as the dust of a graveyard. I cannot bear to remember that awful moment. The judge and the witnesses melted before my eyes. They seemed to disappear like a dream. There, in front of my aching eyes, was the lifeless body of Henry Clerval! I gasped for breath and sank to my knees. 'Have I killed you as well?' I cried. 'You are the third to die because of me. Will there be others?'

My tired body could no longer withstand these shocks. I began to twitch and tremble. I was carried from the room jerking like a puppet in the hands of a madman. At that moment I was totally mad.

22 Fever

I was ill with a fever. I lay for two months on the point of death. My cries were terrible to hear. I called myself the murderer of William, Justine and Clerval. I begged the attendants to help me destroy the monster. I said I felt the fingers of the demon already grasping my neck. I screamed aloud with agony and terror.

Why did I not die? Why did I not sink into that world of everlasting peace? Death snatches away innocent children and turns healthy people into food for worms. Death fills tombs with dust and the smell of rotted bodies. What was so special about me? Why did I not die?

But I was doomed to live. Two months later I recovered my senses. I woke up to find myself in a prison. All around my rough wooden bed were chains and bolts and barred windows. I remembered what had happened and I groaned.

This sound disturbed an old woman who was sleeping in a chair nearby. Her face was rough and hard. There was no pity in her eyes.

'Are you better now, sir?' she said.

'Yes,' I replied, 'but I wish I were dead.'

'I agree with you,' she said. 'All murderers should die.'

How I hated her! I grew feverish again and lost conscious-ness for several hours. When I awoke Mr Kirwin was sitting by my bedside.

'I am sorry this room is so unpleasant,' he said. 'Is there anything I can get you?'

'No. Just let me die. That is all I ask.'

The judge smiled. 'You may soon be free from this place. I am sure some evidence will be found to clear your name.'

'I am not afraid of death.'

Mr Kirwin nodded. 'I know how you feel,' he said. 'You have been very unlucky. It must be a terrible thing to see the dead body of your best friend and then be accused of his murder. I sympathize with you, Mr Frankenstein.'

'How do you know my name?'

'When you were ill, all your papers and letters were brought to me. I wrote to your family two months ago.'

'Are they safe?' I cried. 'Has anyone else been murdered?'

'Your family is perfectly well,' laughed Mr Kirwin, 'and you have a visitor. Shall I show him in?'

For some strange reason I thought this was the monster who had come to mock me in my suffering. I put my hand before my eyes and cried out in agony, 'Oh take him away! I do not want to see him. For God's sake, do not let him enter!'

Mr Kirwin frowned. 'Why do you say that?' he said. 'It is only your father.'

'Then show him in! I am sorry. I thought it was someone else.'

Mr Kirwin nodded and left the room. A moment later my father entered. He tried to cheer me up. He stared at the chains and the barred windows. 'What a strange place this is,' he said. 'Unhappiness seems to follow you around. And poor Clerval——'

'Yes,' I gasped. 'I am cursed. I should have died on the coffin of Henry.'

I fainted once again. When I awoke, my father had gone.

Two weeks later, I was freed from prison. The judge found out that I was in the Orkneys at the time of the murder. I was able to breathe the fresh air again. Soon I would be back in Geneva. But I was not happy. What did it matter to me whether I lived in a dungeon or a palace? The cup of my life was poisoned forever. The sun still continued to shine for other people, but I could not see it. I could see nothing but a dense and frightful darkness and the glimmer of two eyes that glared at me. Sometimes they were the eyes of Henry staring at me from his coffin. Sometimes they were the watery clouded eyes of the monster as I first saw them in my bedroom in Ingoldstadt.

But I decided not to despair. I had a duty to perform. I had to protect my family. I would go back to Geneva and lie in wait for the murderer.

We got on board the ship and sailed away from the shores of Ireland. At midnight I lay on the deck and looked at the stars. I could hear the waves dashing about below me. I was still ill with the fever. My body had become like a skeleton. I kept thinking of Clerval and the death of my brother. I remembered the mad energy with which I had created the demon. A thousand sad thoughts pressed down upon me and I wept.

I was so depressed, I took a double dose of a drug given to me by a doctor. This sent me into a deep sleep. But the drug did not stop me from dreaming. Towards morning I had a kind of nightmare. I felt the monster's hands around my neck. I could not break free. Groans and cries rang in my ears.

I was awoken by my father. I saw the stars above and heard once more the dashing of the waves below. The demon was nowhere to be seen. For the time being I was safe. But for how long?

23   The Marriage

The sea journey came to an end. We landed in France and went to Paris. My father wanted me to meet people. I refused. I was ashamed. I had unchained a monster amongst my fellow human beings. I had set loose a creature who loved more than anything else to spill their blood and laugh with joy at their sufferings and their screams of pain. If they only knew my terrible secret!

My father was getting more and more worried about my behaviour. I would not tell him about the monster, but every so often I kept shouting out that I had killed William, Justine and Henry. This made my father very upset.

'I know you are still ill with the fever,' he said, 'but you must not keep saying those things. It is madness. You must promise never to speak like that again.'

'I am not mad,' I cried. 'The sun and the moon have watched me at work. They know I am telling the truth. I am the killer of those innocent victims. They died because of me. I would have spilled my own blood drop by drop if I could have saved their lives. But I had to think of the whole human race. I could not sacrifice the whole human race!'

My father decided that I was still in a state of shock and quickly changed the subject.

As time passed by, I became more calm. A few weeks later, I was strong enough to leave Paris. On the way to Switzerland I received the following letter from Elizabeth.

My dearest Victor,

I am delighted to hear that you will soon be back in Geneva. Your father tells me how much you have suffered. 受痛苦 *I expect you will be looking even more ill than when you left. I have been very miserable without you. I know that you are still weak from your sickness, but there is something I would like us to talk about very seriously. I must write now while I still have the courage.*

You know that your parents were very anxious to see us married. We were told this when we were quite young. We have always been very affectionate, but perhaps you only look upon me as a kind of sister. Is there somebody else, Victor? I must know the answer to this question. Do you love another?

When you left for England I thought perhaps you were running away from the promise you had made to your parents. I love you, and in my dreams you are always with me. However, if you do not wish to marry me, I will understand.

Do not let this letter disturb you. Don't you answer to-morrow or the next day. If it causes you pain, do not even mention it when we meet. Your father will send me news of your health. If you are happy and smiling I will be overjoyed.

Elizabeth

This letter made me think of the demon's threat, 'I will be with you on your wedding night!' This was my death sentence. On that night the demon would do all he could to destroy me. He would tear me away from all my hopes of happiness. On that night he would end his crimes with my death. Well, let it be so. There would be a fierce and deadly struggle. If he won, I would be at peace and his power over me would end. If he lost, I would be a free man. A free man! I gave a bitter laugh. I would be as free as a peasant who has seen his family murdered before his eyes and his cottage burned. I would still be guilty of the death of three people. The only advantage I would gain from victory would be the love of Elizabeth.

I read Elizabeth's letter again and again. I loved her with all my heart. I would die to make her happy. I remembered that the monster had promised to be with me on my wedding night. Supposing I did not marry? The monster would still continue to murder and destroy. After all, he had killed Clerval. What had I to lose? Better to get it over with. With these thoughts in mind, I wrote a letter:

My dearest Elizabeth,

*You are the only hope of happiness that is left to me.
I love you dearly and we will be married as soon as
possible. But I have a secret, Elizabeth. It is a dreadful
secret. When I tell you about it, your body will go cold
with horror. You will not be surprised that I have been so
unhappy. I will tell you this secret the day after our
marriage. Until then you must not say a single word on
this subject to me or anybody else.*

Your future husband,
Victor

One week later my father and I returned to Geneva. Elizabeth welcomed me with warm affection, but there were tears
in her eyes as well. She saw that my body had almost turned
into a skeleton and my cheeks were filled with fever.

To my horror, I began to have fits of real madness. Sometimes I would blaze with fury and shout out in a loud voice.
Sometimes I would sit in a corner and speak to nobody. It
was only the kindness of Elizabeth that kept bringing me
back to sanity.

The date fixed for our wedding drew nearer. My heart
began to sink inside me but I pretended to be happy and
cheerful. I began to arm myself in case the demon should
make his attack. I carried pistols and a dagger wherever I
went. I was beginning to feel safer.

During the wedding, Elizabeth became very sad as if somehow she knew that evil was waiting round the corner. Perhaps
she was worried about my secret.

After the ceremony, Elizabeth and I set off on our honeymoon. We hired a boat and began to sail across the lake.

Those were the last moments of my life in which I enjoyed
the feeling of happiness. The boat moved quickly. The sun
was hot but we were sheltered by a sail. The scenery was
truly beautiful. There were snow-covered mountains and
lovely green trees by the shore. Small birds sang as they flew
overhead.

I took Elizabeth's hand. 'Why are you so sad?' I asked. 'We will not live forever. We should be happy while we can.'

'Don't worry about me,' she replied. 'Deep down I am very happy. But there is a voice that keeps whispering to me. I will not listen to that voice any longer. Look,' she said, 'see how fast the clouds are passing overhead. I can see the top of the alps. Look down there! Can you not see all those fish swimming in the clear waters? I can see every stone that lies at the bottom!'

Elizabeth tried to look cheerful, but in her eyes I saw the shadows of fear. I too was afraid.

The sun sank lower in the heavens. We passed into a river and sailed towards a small village. We saw the spire of a church shine beneath the wooded slopes of hills. As we approached the shore, the soft wind wafted the delightful scent of flowers and hay towards us. The sun sank beneath the horizon and once again my heart began to freeze with fear.

24 The Monster Keeps His Promise

It was eight o'clock when we landed. We walked for a short time on the shore. Then we went into the garden of a nearby inn. We spent a long time looking at the beauty of the waters, woods and mountains.

But the wind began to rise. It became more and more violent. Clouds were swept across the moon. Large waves began to ruffle the surface of the lake. Suddenly a heavy storm of rain fell down from the heavens.

I had been calm during the day. But when night came, a thousand fears entered my mind. I was anxious and watchful. I kept my right hand firmly gripped on a pistol hidden beneath my jacket. Every sound terrified me. I was ready to fight for my life. I would not stop fighting until my enemy had been killed.

Elizabeth watched me. She remained silent at first, but then she began to tremble. 'What's the matter, Victor?' she asked. 'What are you frightened of?'

'Please don't ask questions, my love,' I replied. 'If I survive this night, all will be safe. But this night is dreadful, very dreadful.'

An hour passed by. The demon could strike at any moment. I did not want Elizabeth to get hurt in the fighting, so I told her to go to bed. Then I walked through the passages of the house looking for the monster. But I could not find any trace of him. I began to think that something had happened to the creature. It was then that I heard a shrill and dreadful scream. It came from the room in which Elizabeth had gone to bed. As soon as I heard this sound I realized the truth. I must have been blind! The demon had outwitted me. My arms dropped in horror. Every muscle in my body seemed to freeze. This state lasted only a fraction of a second before I snapped out of my trance. There came a

second scream. I rushed into the room.

Great God! The sight almost killed me. There was Elizabeth thrown across the bed like a broken doll. Her body was pale and lifeless. Her head hung downwards. The face was twisted out of shape with pain and her dead eyes stared upwards at the ceiling. Everywhere I go, I see that picture. I see her white, bloodless arms dangling to the floor. My head seemed to explode and I fell to the ground.

When I recovered, I found myself surrounded by the people of the inn. Their faces were breathless with horror. I staggered to my feet and ran to the room where the corpse of Elizabeth was now to be found. She had been placed on a table. Her head was placed upon her arm and a handkerchief was thrown across her face and neck. It seemed as though she were sleeping. I rushed over to her and kissed her. But she was cold. The woman I had loved was no more. The marks of the murderer's fingers were on her neck and no breath came from her lips.

While I still hung to her in an agony of despair, I happened to look up. I saw a pale yellow moon shining through the window. The shutters had been thrown back. At the open window stood the huge, terrifying shape of the monster. A twisted grin was on his face. He seemed to be laughing. He pointed with his hellish finger at the corpse of my wife. I rushed to the window and took the pistol from my jacket and fired. But he escaped me. He ran with the speed of lightning and plunged into the lake.

The sound of the pistol brought a crowd into the room. I pointed to the spot where he had disappeared. We followed the track with boats. Nets were thrown, but they caught nothing. Several hours later we returned. Then we began to search the woods of the surrounding countryside.

I wanted to go with them. I started to walk towards a forest, but my head began to spin around and around. My steps were like those of a drunken man. I fell down at last in a state of utter exhaustion. A mist covered my eyes and my skin was burned dry with the heart of fever. In this state I was carried back and placed on a bed. My eyes kept wandering around the room as if looking for something that I had lost.

Some time later, I got up and went back to the room where the body of Elizabeth lay. There were women weeping around her. My mind was completely numb. I just stared at the body and thought of William, Justine and Clerval. I shuddered. At this very moment, my father might be twisting around in the grasp of the demon! Was he too to be taken from me? Was I to be left with nothing?

I decided to return to Geneva with all possible speed.

25 The Demon Escapes

There were no horses so I had to return by the lake. I hired two men to row. At first the wind was fierce and the rain was very heavy. Gradually, however, the sun came out. I saw the fish play in the waters as they had done a few hours before. I remembered Elizabeth pointing them out.

When I arrived at Geneva, I found that my father had heard the bad news. He had become seriously ill. Three days later he died of a broken heart. I was now all alone in the world. I was filled with a terrible and burning rage. I wanted revenge. I would destroy the monster. I would destroy this thing of evil that I had created with my own hateful hands.

I told my story to a judge. I wanted him to send out a search party. The judge listened to my story in amazement. He thought I was crazy or sick with the fever. He refused to help me. This was what I had expected. did not believe him.

I collected together a large sum of money and some jewels. Then I began to search for clues. I spent hours wandering about the neighbourhood. My task seemed hopeless. I was in despair. The monster could be many, many miles away by now. When night fell, I found myself outside the cemetery. This was the place where William, Elizabeth and my father had been buried. I entered it and stared at the tomb which marked their graves. Everything was silent except the leaves of the trees which were gently shaken by the wind. The night was nearly dark and the air was filled with sadness. The ghosts of the dead seemed to fly around and make shadows.

My misery gave way to anger and frustration. They were dead and I was living. Their murderer was still alive and had not yet been punished. I knelt on the grass and kissed the earth. My lips trembled and I spoke out loud. 'By the sacred earth on which I kneel and by the ghosts all around, I swear that I will find this murdering demon and destroy him. While there is still a drop of life left in my body I will hunt him down. Let this monster be cursed. Let him feel the misery he has caused to others!'

Suddenly, through the stillness of the night, came a loud and hellish laugh. It rang in my ears and my blood went cold. The laughter died away and I heard a loud whisper close to my ear. 'I am satisfied. Miserable wretch! You have decided to live and I am satisfied.'

I rushed to the spot where the sound had come from, but the devil escaped from me. Suddenly the wide circle of the moon arose. It shone upon his ghost-like shape as he ran away with a speed no living creature could match.

The chase was on!

追踪

26 The Long Chase

I have followed him for many months. My travels took me to
the blue Mediterranean and then on to the Black Sea. I
chased him across the wilds of Mongolia and Russia, but he
escaped from me. Sometimes terrified peasants told me of
the demon who had passed through their district. Sometimes
the monster left tracks. The snows fell on my head and I saw
the print of his huge foot on the white plain. I suffered from
cold, hunger and weariness. I was kept alive only by my
burning desire for revenge.

I do not know what the feelings of the demon were. Sometimes he left messages carved in the bark of trees or engraved
them in blocks of stone. There were such messages as:

'My reign is not yet over.

'You are still alive, and my power is complete. I am taking
you to the everlasting ice of the north. You will feel the
misery of cold and frost which cannot harm me. Near to this
place you will find a dead hare. Eat it and be refreshed. Come
on my enemy! We have yet to fight for our lives. You will
have to live through many hard and miserable hours before
that moment will arrive.'

The mocking devil! May he suffer endless torture and
death. I will never give up my search until one of us dies.
Then I will join Elizabeth and my family in the garden of
paradise.

The demon took me further and further northwards. The
snows became thicker and the weather became almost too
cold to bear. The peasants shut themselves up in their huts
while their animals died of starvation. The rivers became
covered with ice and no fish could be obtained.

My enemy became more and more confident as my sufferings increased. One of his inscriptions read as follows:

'Prepare yourself! Your hardships have only just begun.

Wrap yourself in furs and provide yourself with food. We shall soon begin a journey where your sufferings will satisfy my everlasting hatred.'

These scoffing words only increased my determination. I continued to cross huge deserts of snow until at last the ocean appeared in the distance. How unlike the blue seas of the south was this! It was completely covered with ice. It was almost impossible to tell where the land ended and the ice began. This, I hoped, was the place where I was to do battle with the demon.

Some weeks before sighting this frozen ocean, I had obtained a sledge and some dogs. I had been able to cross the snows with tremendous speed. Gradually, I began to catch up with the monster. I had hoped to catch him before he reached the sea.

I continued my journey and arrived at a tiny collection of huts by the shore. The people who lived there told me that a huge monster had arrived the night before. He had been armed with a gun and many pistols. This creature had frightened away the inhabitant of one of the huts and stolen all their store of winter food. Then he had placed it on a sledge and grabbed hold of a team of well-trained dogs. To the joy of the villagers, he had set off across the frozen sea in a direction that led to no land. There, he would be destroyed, they said, by the breaking up of the ice or be frozen to death by the everlasting frosts.

This information filled me with despair. He had escaped me yet again! I would have to journey across the frozen sea. I would have to face a cold that no man had ever faced before. But the thought of the demon escaping unpunished for his murders filled me with hatred. The spirits of the dead seemed to hover round me begging for their revenge. I slept for a while then I began the chase yet again.

I bought a large supply of food and a sledge which would travel more easily across the icy hills of the frozen sea. When all was ready, I set off from the land.

I don't know how many days passed since that moment.

I travelled on and on. I crossed huge mountains of jagged ice. I almost lost the use of my toes through frostbite. Once, the ice opened up before me and I was almost swallowed up by the sea. My supply of food grew smaller and smaller.

One of the dogs died at the top of a steep mountain. I stopped. I was just about to give up all hope when I saw a speck upon the snow. When I realized what it was, I uttered a wild cry of joy. I saw a sledge and the huge, distorted shape of the demon.

I followed the speck for two days. All the time I was catching it up. Soon my enemy would be in my grasp. My eyes were filled with tears of joy.

But it was not to be! Suddenly I heard the sea move beneath the ice. The thunder of the rolling waters became louder and louder. I pressed on, but in vain. The wind rose and the sea roared. There was a sudden shudder like that of an earthquake. The ice split and cracked before my eyes. In a few minutes the sea was rolling between me and my enemy. I was left drifting on a piece of ice which kept growing smaller. Soon I would plunge to my death in the icy waters.

Many hours passed. Several of my dogs died. I was almost ready to fall into the sleep of death when I saw your ship. I destroyed part of my sledge and made myself some oars. Then I began to row my raft of ice in the direction of your vessel. I came on board only because you were going north-wards in the direction of the demon. If you had been going to the south, I would have remained on my raft of ice in the hope that God would guide me towards my enemy.

I feel I will soon die and the monster will still live. If you meet him, Captain Walton, you must promise not to let him escape. He will destroy others. He is a murderer who cannot be trusted. Do not listen to his persuasive words. He is full of cunning and his soul is as hellish as his appearance. When he talks, remember the names of William, Justine, Clerval, Elizabeth, my father, and myself, the wretched Victor Frankenstein. Plunge your sword into his black heart. My ghost will hover near you and direct the blade . . .

Letters Written by Robert Walton to His Sister, Margaret

August 23rd

Now you will have read this terrifying story, Margaret. Has it frozen your blood with horror? I know the monster truly exists. But where is he now? Perhaps we will meet him on our journey to the North Pole.

I tried to find out how Frankenstein made this creature, but he refuses to reveal his secret. 'Are you mad?' he said. 'Do you also wish to create a demon that will destroy you? Do you wish to create a monster that will terrorize the world? You must learn from my mistakes.'

September 2nd

My beloved sister,

We are all in great danger, I fear I may never see England again. We are surrounded by mountains of ice. There is no way past them and each moment they threaten to crush the ship. The crew are frightened. Frankenstein offers me comfort and tries to persuade the men not to despair. For a while he persuades them that the mountains of ice are like molehills and will disappear if they remain brave. But the men are still very restless. I fear there will be a mutiny.

September 5th

We are still surrounded by mountains of ice. The weather is becoming colder and colder. Several of my comrades have already died. Frankenstein is growing weaker all the time. A fever burns in his eyes and he is easily exhausted by any action.

This morning, as I sat watching the white face of my friend, six sailors came into my cabin. They wanted me to promise to return home if we succeeded in escaping from the mountains of ice.

I was about to reply when Frankenstein propped himself up on a pillow and spoke. 'What do you mean?' he said, speaking to the men. 'You came here looking for glory. You wanted to be explorers. You wanted to be remembered forever by the human race. You knew there would be danger. Are you going to be defeated by the first obstacle you meet? Do you want to bring shame to your captain and show the world that you are cowards? You must have courage. You must remain as firm as a rock. The ice will disappear. It is not as strong as your hearts. Don't return to your families as failures. Return as heroes who have fought and conquered and have never turned their backs upon the enemy.'

The crew looked at one another. They were embarrassed. I told them to think matters over. If they still wanted to go home I would agree. But I hoped they would be filled with courage and continue.

The men left. I looked at my friend. He was now unconscious. The effort of the speech had been too much for him.

I fear that the men will demand to return home. I am filled with shame. My dreams of glory are already beginning to fade. It is as though a part of my soul had died.

September 7th

It is all over. The men have reached their decision. I have agreed to return if we are not destroyed by the ice. My hopes have been shattered by their cowardice. I will return as a failure.

September 12th

The expedition has come to an end. I have lost my dreams of honour and glory. I have lost my friend. I am returning to England. I will write to tell you how it happened as the wind blows the ship back towards land. Perhaps this will help take my mind off the bitter feelings of failure and disappointment which fill my heart.

On September 9th the ice began to move. Roars like thunder were heard in the distance. Islands of ice split and cracked in every direction. We were in terrible danger, but we could do nothing but wait. I sat by the side of my friend who was on the point of death. The ice cracked behind us and it was driven towards the north with tremendous force. A breeze came from the west and on September 11th the passage towards the south became perfectly free. When the sailors saw this, they gave a terrific shout of joy. It was loud and continued a long, long time. Frankenstein woke up.

'Why are they shouting?' he asked.

'They shout because they will soon return to England.'

'Is this true?'

'Yes,' I replied. 'I can't make them change their minds. I must return with them.'

'You may return,' he said, 'but I will go on. I have a job to do. I dare not fail. I am weak but the spirits who demand my revenge will give me strength.' Having said this, he tried to jump out of his bed. But the effort was too great for him. He fell back and fainted.

It was a long time before he came back to life. At last, though, he opened his eyes. He breathed with difficulty and was unable to speak. The ship's doctor gave him a sleeping drug and ordered me not to disturb him. He told me that my friend did not have many hours left to live.

I sat by Frankenstein's bed and watched him. His eyes were closed and I thought he was asleep. Then I heard a feeble voice. He was asking me to come near. He wanted me to hear what he had to say.

'Alas!' he said. 'My strength has gone. I feel that I will soon die and my enemy will remain alive. I have been thinking about the past. I created this demon in a fit of mad enthusiasm and watched him turn against the human race. He became totally evil. He destroyed my friends. He hates all those happier than himself. I do not know when his thirst for revenge will end. It was my duty to destroy him, but I have failed. He still lives and this worries me. Otherwise, I am happy to die. It is the first real happiness I have known for years. I can see the forms of my dead friends moving in

front of my eyes. They fly like angels, and I must hurry to their arms. Farewell, Walton! Be happy. Enjoy a peaceful life and don't be ambitious. Scientific discoveries can be very dangerous. Yet why do I say this? My hopes have been destroyed, perhaps another man may succeed.'

His voice became fainter as he spoke. At length he became exhausted and sank into silence. Half an hour later he tried to speak again, but he was not able to do so. I saw his eyes close forever and a gentle smile disappeared slowly from his lips.

What else is there to say, Margaret? I have lost a friend and I return home full of disappointment. Perhaps, however, I will find some kind of happiness in England.

I am interrupted. What are these sounds that I hear? It is midnight. The breeze is blowing and the watchmen on deck are silent. Again I hear it! It is like the sound of a human voice, but hoarser. It comes from the cabin where the dead body of Frankenstein still lies. I must get up and investigate. Good night, my sister.

Great God! What a scene has just taken place! The memory of it still makes me dizzy. I have hardly the strength left to tell you about it.

I entered the cabin where my friend's body was. Standing over him was a shape so horrible I can hardly describe it! It was a giant with a deformed, twisted body. As he hung over the coffin his face was hidden by long locks of ragged hair. He held out one huge hand which was slippery and green. When he heard me, he stopped groaning and jumped towards the window. Never had I seen such terrifying ugliness. I shut my eyes in disgust.

But the monster did not jump through the window. He remained where he was and turned towards the dead man. His huge body shook like a storm.

'That is also my victim!' he roared. 'His murder is the end of my work. My miseries are now over. Oh Frankenstein! If you were alive, I would beg your forgiveness. But it is too late. You are cold and you cannot hear me!'

His voice was choked with feeling. I was curious and felt

rather sorry for this creature. I came nearer but I did not
lift my eyes to look at his hideous face. I tried to speak but
my words died away on my lips. The monster continued to
groan and call himself names. At length I gained enough
courage to talk to him.

'It is too late to be sorry,' I said. 'If you had been less
keen on revenge, Frankenstein would be still alive.'

'Do you think I enjoyed doing what I did?' he replied.
'I was torn between my desire for revenge and my guilty
conscience. I hated myself for those murders. Do you think
the groans of Clerval were music to my ears?'

'You are being false,' I said. 'Frankenstein warned me that
you were a cunning liar. You are like those people who throw
torches into buildings and then sit amongst the ruins pre-
tending to cry. If Frankenstein were still alive you would
carry on torturing him and making his life a misery. You
would still want your revenge. It is not pity you feel. You
are only sorry because you have no one left to hurt.'

The monster interrupted me. 'That is not true!' he cried.
'I am not asking you for your sympathy. Nobody has shown
me any sort of kindness in my life. I was once full of love
for the human race. Now I hate all mankind. I am like an
angel who has turned into a devil. The world is my hell and I
am completely alone.

'Frankenstein has told you of his own sufferings, but he
has not told you of mine. All the time I desired love and
affection and I received none. I have sinned against mankind,
but mankind has sinned against me. If you hate me, why do
you not hate Frankenstein and the cottagers for what they
did to me? Why do you not hate the farmer who shot me
when I had saved his child?

'But it is true that I have become evil. I have murdered the
lovely and the helpless. I have strangled the innocent as they
slept. I have grabbed the throats and killed those who never
did me any harm. And I have caused the death of my creator.
There he lies, white and cold in death. You hate me, and I
hate myself. My life has been filled with nothing but misery.

'But I will do no more evil. My work is complete. I shall leave your ship and go back to the ice raft that brought me here. Then I will go to the most northern part of the earth and burn myself to ashes. I shall no longer feel the agonies and frustrations of my wretched life. I shall no longer see the sun or stars or feel the winds play on my cheeks. Death is the only happiness I will have ever known.

'Farewell! You are the last person who will ever see me alive. I will rejoice in the agony of the flames. My ashes will be swept into the sea by the winds. Perhaps my spirit will sleep in peace. Farewell!'

As he said this, he jumped from the cabin window. He landed upon the ice raft which lay close to the ship. Soon he was carried away by the waves and lost in the darkness and distance.

Questions

Robert Walton meets Frankenstein

1. To whom does Robert Walton write his letters? *Margaret* *his siste*
2. To what place is Robert Walton leading his expedition? *North Pole*
3. How does Robert Walton's ship become trapped?
4. How did Robert Walton refuse to allow the sailors to follow the giant?
5. Explain how Robert Walton first met the man called Frankenstein.
6. Why had Frankenstein travelled so far over the ice?

A thick fog surrounded the ship, and there is not any water for the ship to float.

The Story of Frankenstein

Chapter 1
1. Where was Frankenstein born? *switzerland*
2. How did Elizabeth become a part of Frankenstein's family? *Because Frankenstein's mother adopted her*
3. What was the name of Frankenstein's brother? *William*
4. What incident made Frankenstein interested in electricity? *The thunder storm*

Chapter 2
1. How did Frankenstein's mother die? *scarlet fever*
2. What subject did Professor Waldman teach? *modern Chem*
3. How did Frankenstein get the dead bodies he used for his experiments?
4. What secret did Frankenstein discover?
5. Why did Frankenstein feel he was working too hard?

Chapter 3
1. What happens when Frankenstein sends the first spark of life into the creature?
2. Why had the creature become so ugly?
3. Why does Frankenstein faint? *智迷*
4. Describe Frankenstein's nightmare.

I saw the dull yellow eye of the creature open, it breath hardly and a deep and deep shadows

5. What does Frankenstein see when he recovers consciousness?

6. How tall was the monster?

7. Frankenstein runs away to a friend's house. Who is this friend?

8. Why is Frankenstein so happy when he first gets back to his room?

9. Why does Frankenstein faint again?

Chapter 4
1. How long did Frankenstein's fever last?

2. What are Frankenstein's feelings about science now?

3. What is the name of the servant girl hired by Elizabeth?

Chapter 5
1. How was Frankenstein's brother killed?

2. Why does Elizabeth blame herself for William's death?

Chapter 6
1. What is the name of the mountain near lake Geneva?

2. Who does Frankenstein see at the side of the lake?

3. Why doesn't Frankenstein tell the police who the murderer is?

4. Why do people believe Justine Moritz killed William?

5. Why doesn't Frankenstein tell Elizabeth and his father the truth?

Chapter 7
1. What does Elizabeth say about Justine Moritz at the trial?

2. What was the verdict of the jury?

Chapter 8
1. How did the priest persuade Justine to confess to the murder?

2. Explain why Frankenstein blames himself for the death of William and Justine.

Chapter 9
1. Describe the scenery in the alps.

2. Why is the monster so unhappy?

3. What does the monster threaten to do?

4. Why does the monster look upon Frankenstein as a kind of god?

The Story of the Monster

Chapter 10
1. What was the first food of the monster?
2. What does the monster do when he comes to the fire left by the beggars?

Chapter 11
1. What does the old man do when he sees the monster?
2. How do the villagers force the monster to go away?
3. Where does the monster hide? *hovel*

Chapter 12
1. How does the monster know what is happening inside the house?
2. What are the feelings of the monster when he sees the old man kiss the little girl?
3. How did the monster know he was so ugly?
4. Where does the monster practise speaking?
5. How does the monster learn to read?
6. What does the monster learn about God and the Devil?
7. How does the monster learn that he was made by Frankenstein?
8. Why does the monster keep thinking of Adam and Eve?

Chapter 13
1. What happens when the monster shows himself to the family?
2. Do you think the monster acted wisely?

Chapter 14
1. What do the family say to the landlord of their house? *They said that their home was haunted by a demon*
2. What does the monster do when the family have left? *He felt very despair and destroy the vegetables in the garden*

Chapter 15
1. Explain how the monster saves a little girl.
2. How is the monster rewarded for his good deed?
　　　　　　報 仇

Chapter 16
1. Why does the monster want to capture the little boy? *He want to teach the boy to love and respect him.*
2. What does the boy say to the monster and why does this make the monster so angry?
3. Why does the monster kill the boy? How does he do it? *He want to silent him. He squeezed his throat*

4. What does the monster find around the boy's neck?
5. Where does the monster find the sleeping woman?

Justine Moritz

6. Who is this sleeping woman? What does the monster do whilst she is asleep?
7. What does the monster want Frankenstein to do for him?

The Story of Frankenstein (Continued)

Chapter 17

1. How does the monster threaten Frankenstein? 恐嚇
2. How does the monster make Frankenstein feel guilty?
3. Where does the monster say he will go if Frankenstein makes him a mate? *South America*
4. Why is Frankenstein so suspicious of the monster? *Because the monster had kill a lot of people*
5. Why does Frankenstein finally agree to help the monster? *He will continue to kill*
6. What does Frankenstein make the monster promise to do?

Chapter 18

1. Why does Frankenstein's father want him to marry Elizabeth quickly?
2. Why does Frankenstein travel to England?
3. Who keeps Frankenstein company on his journey?
4. Where does Frankenstein go in order to start making a female monster? *Orkneys*
5. Describe the scenery in this place. How is it so different from Switzerland?

Chapter 19

1. Why does Frankenstein think it might be wrong to make a female monster? Give as many different reasons as you can.
2. Whose face does Frankenstein see looking through the window? *the monster*
3. What is there about this face that makes Frankenstein realise his mistake?
4. What does Frankenstein do when he sees the face?
5. On what day does the monster threaten to visit Frankenstein again?

Frankenstein's wedding night

clerval

Chapter 20 1. Who sends Frankenstein a letter from Switzerland?
2. What does Frankenstein throw into the sea? Why does he do this?
3. What happens to Frankenstein's boat?
4. Where does the boat finally arrive? *Ireland*
5. Why is Frankenstein taken to Judge Kirwin?

Chapter 21 1. How had a young man been murdered the previous night?
2. Who was the murdered man? *clerval*
3. What effect has the sight of the dead man on Frankenstein?

Chapter 22 1. How long was Frankenstein in a fever? *two months*
2. Where does Frankenstein find himself when he recovers?
3. Who came to visit Frankenstein in prison? *his father*
4. Why was Frankenstein released?

Chapter 23 1. Why does Elizabeth think Frankenstein went to England?
2. What does Frankenstein think will happen to him on his wedding night? *the monster would kill him*
3. What are Frankenstein's feelings towards Elizabeth?
4. What does Frankenstein carry about with him for protection? *pistols dagger*
5. Where do Frankenstein and Elizabeth go on their honeymoon? *a lake*

Chapter 24 1. How does the monster get his revenge? *The monster grasp kill*
2. Describe the terrible scene that Frankenstein sees in the bedroom.
3. Where does Frankenstein suddenly see the monster? What does the monster do?

Chapter 25 1. How does Frankenstein's father die?
2. What is the reaction of the judge when Frankenstein tells him about the monster?
3. What does Frankenstein decide to do about the monster? *to destroy it.*

Chapter 26   1. Where does the monster lead Frankenstein? *North Pole*
     2. How did Frankenstein almost lose his toes?
     3. What prevented Frankenstein from finally catching up with the monster?
     4. At first Frankenstein would not come on board Robert Walton's ship. Why did he change his mind?

The Death of Frankenstein

     1. Why does Frankenstein refuse to tell Robert Walton how he made the monster?
     2. What do the crew force Robert Walton to do? Why are the crew so worried?
     3. Why is Frankenstein glad to die?
     4. Why is the monster so sad to see that Frankenstein is dead?
     5. Why does the monster hate himself?
     6. How does the monster plan to kill himself?

1. It is because Frankenstein afraid that Robert will creat a terrible monster too.

OXFORD PROGRESSIVE ENGLISH READERS

GRADE 1

Vocabulary restricted to 1900 head words
Illustrated in two and partly in full colours
One illustration every 6 pages on average

The Adventures of Hang Tuah	MUBIN SHEPPARD
Alice's Adventures in Wonderland	LEWIS CARROLL
A Christmas Carol	CHARLES DICKENS
Don Quixote	CERVANTES
Great Expectations	CHARLES DICKENS
Gulliver's Travels	JONATHAN SWIFT
The House of Sixty Fathers	MEINDERT DEJONG
Islands in the Sky	ARTHUR C. CLARKE
Jane Eyre	CHARLOTTE BRONTË
Little Women	LOUISA M. ALCOTT
Madam White Snake	RETOLD BY BENJAMIN CHIA
Oliver Twist	CHARLES DICKENS
Plays for Malaysian Schools I	PATRICK YEOH
The Stone Junk	RETOLD BY D.H. HOWE
Stories of Shakespeare's Plays I	RETOLD BY N. KATES
The Tale of the Bounty	RETOLD BY H.G. WYATT
Tales from Tolstoy	RETOLD BY R.D. BINFIELD
Tales of Si Kabayan	MURTAGH MURPHY
The Talking Tree & Other Stories	DAVID McROBBIE
The Tiger of Lembah Pahit	NORMA R. YOUNGBERG
A Time of Darkness	SHAMUS FRAZER
Treasure Island	R.L. STEVENSON

GRADE 2

Vocabulary restricted to 2900 head words
One two-coloured illustration every 10 pages on average

The Adventures of Tom Sawyer	MARK TWAIN
Around the World in Eighty Days	JULES VERNE
Asia Pacific Stories	MURTAGH MURPHY
Chinese Tales of the Supernatural	RETOLD BY BENJAMIN CHIA
The Crocodile Dies Twice	SHAMUS FRAZER
David Copperfield	CHARLES DICKENS
Five Tales	OSCAR WILDE
Fog & Other Stories	BILL LOWE
The Hound of the Baskervilles	SIR ARTHUR CONAN DOYLE
The Missing Scientist	S.F. STEVENS
Plays for Malaysian Schools II	PATRICK YEOH
Robinson Crusoe	DANIEL DEFOE
Seven Chinese Stories	T.J. SHERIDAN
Stories of Shakespeare's Plays II	RETOLD BY WYATT & FULLERTON
A Tale of Two Cities	CHARLES DICKENS
Tales of Crime & Detection	RETOLD BY G.F. WEAR
Two Boxes of Gold & Other Stories	CHARLES DICKENS
Two Famous English Comedies	RETOLD BY RICHARD CROFT
Vanity Fair	W.M. THACKERAY

GRADE 3

Vocabulary restricted to 3500 head words
One two-coloured illustration every 15 pages on average

Animal Farm	GEORGE ORWELL
Battle of Wits at Crimson Cliff	RETOLD BY BENJAMIN CHIA
Dr Jekyll & Mr Hyde & Other Stories	R.L. STEVENSON
From Russia, with Love	IAN FLEMING
The Gifts & Other Stories	O. HENRY & OTHERS
Journey to the Centre of the Earth	JULES VERNE
Kidnapped	R.L. STEVENSON
King Solomon's Mines	H. RIDER HAGGARD
Lady Precious Stream	S.I. HSIUNG
The Light of Day	ERIC AMBLER
The Mask of Dimitrios	ERIC AMBLER
Moonraker	IAN FLEMING
The Moonstone	WILKIE COLLINS
A Night of Terror & Other Strange Tales	GUY DE MAUPASSANT
The Red Winds	SHAMUS FRAZER
Seven Stories	H.G. WELLS
Stories of Shakespeare's Plays III	RETOLD BY H.G. WYATT
Tales of Mystery & Imagination	EDGAR ALLAN POE
The War of the Worlds	H.G. WELLS
20,000 Leagues under the Sea	JULES VERNE
The Woman in White	WILKIE COLLINS
Wuthering Heights	EMILY BRONTË
You Only Live Twice	IAN FLEMING

GRADE 4

Vocabulary restricted to 5000 head words
One two-coloured illustration every 15 pages on average

Frankenstein	MARY SHELLEY
The Mayor of Casterbridge	THOMAS HARDY
Pride and Prejudice	JANE AUSTEN